50 WALKS IN

Edinburgh &
Eastern Scotland

50 WALKS OF 2–10 MILES

Contents

Contents

Rating

Each walk is rated for its relative difficulty compared to the other walks in this book. Walks marked ✚✚✚ are likely to be shorter and easier with little total ascent. The hardest walks are marked ✚✚✚.

Walking in Safety

For advice and safety tips see page 144.

Locator Map

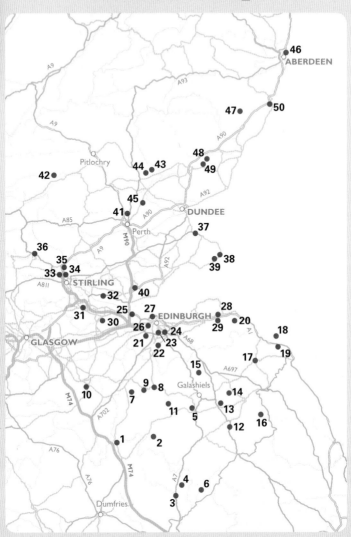

Legend

--→--	Walk Route		▨	Built-up Area
❶	Route Waypoint		▨	Woodland Area
-- -- --	Adjoining Path		🛉🛉	Toilet
⚡	Viewpoint		P	Car Park
•	Place of Interest		🍱	Picnic Area
⛰	Steep Section		)(	Bridge

Introducing Edinburgh & Eastern Scotland

The glen was deserted. The only sounds I could hear were the chattering of the river and the whisper of the summer wind. I took the path that ran uphill from the sleepy little church, and followed it as it snaked its way on to the moors. The heather was in bloom, quilting the lonely uplands in a bouncy blanket of purple, amethyst and mauve. I walked briskly, breathing in the crystal air – unaccompanied save for the occasional skylark or delicately painted butterfly. In the distance rose a range of hills, their sides etched with craggy rocks that had been weathered by thousands of years of ice, and snow, and rain. Eventually I reached a sheepfold, a neat circle of deep grey stones that had been hewn into blocks by unknown hands and somehow carried on to this isolated moor. This would be a harsh place in winter – but in summer it was a delight…

There are lots of places like this in eastern Scotland – places where you can escape the crowds and walk through countryside that still seems to belong to nature rather than man. Too few people explore this part of Scotland, at least on foot, as they seem to feel that walking in Scotland means the Highlands. Of course, it's true that the Highlands offer the wildest walking – but the variety, the history and the coastline of the east are more than adequate compensation.

Walking For All

This is a vast area and encompasses a deliciously varied range of landscapes: you'll find everything from historic cobbled streets in Edinburgh to narrow sheep tracks on the Eildon Hills. There is walking here to suit all tastes and abilities, whether you like a gentle ramble through the fields or a strenuous hike up a hill. There are plenty of footpaths and a number of waymarked, long distance trails cut through the countryside. You can follow sections of the Southern Upland Way, which runs 212 miles (341km) from Portpatrick in the west to Cockburnspath in the east; the Pennine Way (270 miles/435km) which has its northern terminus at Kirk Yetholm in the Borders; and St Cuthbert's Way (62 miles/100km) from Melrose to Lindisfarne. You can also follow old drove roads or walk along Dere Street, an old Roman road.

Landscapes of Character

The scenery here shows surprising variations in character. The rolling hills of the south-west feel remote and lonely, while the borderlands to the east have a pastoral appeal, dominated by the mighty Tweed and dotted with mature trees and historic abbeys like Dryburgh and Melrose. The coastline is different again, with dark sandy beaches and dramatic cliffs that support colonies of seabirds.

PUBLIC TRANSPORT

Many walks in this book are only accessible by car. However, there are regular train services from Edinburgh to Stirling, Dunblane, Linlithgow, Falkirk and Perth. For national rail enquiries, phone 0845 748 4950 or visit www.nationalrail.co.uk; for Scottish Citylink (bus and coach) phone 08705 505050 or visit www.citylink.co.uk; for Traveline phone 0871 200 2233 or visit www.traveline.org.uk.

Exploring the Area

Not only are the streets of Edinburgh picturesque and full of history, it is also surrounded by the Pentland Hills. From here, you cross the Forth Bridge to the ancient kingdom of Fife, and can follow the Coastal Path, which runs through pretty fishing villages like Anstruther and Crail. West of Fife is the heart of Scotland – Perthshire, where the landscape becomes wilder. This is the Scotland of dreams, with moody castles and brooding hills. The north-east is different again. In Angus you can explore peaceful glens, such as Glen Prosen, or visit Kirriemuir, where J M Barrie, Peter Pan's creator, was born. Further north is the Howe of the Mearns, immortalised in the books of Lewis Grassic Gibbon; and then – well, get those boots on and find out...

Using this book

Information panels

An information panel for each walk shows its relative difficulty (see page 5), the distance and total amount of ascent. An indication of the gradients you will encounter is shown by the rating ▲ ▲ ▲ (no steep slopes) to ▲ ▲ ▲ (several very steep slopes).

Maps

There are 30 maps, covering 40 of the walks. Some walks have a suggested option in the same area. The information panel for these walks will tell you how much extra walking is involved. On short-cut suggestions the panel will tell you the total distance if you set out from the start of the main walk. Where an option returns to the same point on the main walk, just the distance of the loop is given. Where an option leaves the main walk at one point and returns to it at another, then the distance shown is for the whole walk. The minimum time suggested is for reasonably fit walkers and doesn't allow for stops. Each walk has a suggested map.

Start Points

The start of each walk is given as a six-figure grid reference prefixed by two letters indicating which 100km square of the National Grid it refers to. You'll find more information on grid references on most Ordnance Survey maps.

Dogs

We have tried to give dog owners useful advice about how dog friendly each walk is. Please respect other countryside users. Keep your dog under control, especially around livestock, and obey local bylaws and other dog control notices.

Car Parking

Many of the car parks suggested are public, but occasionally you may find you have to park on the roadside or in a lay-by. Please be considerate when you leave your car, ensuring that access roads or gates are not blocked and that other vehicles can pass safely.

Right: Foxgloves in the Den of Alyth (Walk 44)

A Beefy Devil of a Walk in Moffat

A hearty walk around the intriguingly named Devil's Beef Tub near the small town of Moffat.

DISTANCE 4.5 miles (7.2km)   **MINIMUM TIME** 2hrs

ASCENT/GRADIENT 1,076ft (328m) ▲▲▲   **LEVEL OF DIFFICULTY** +++

PATHS Farm tracks, small paths; narrow path across steep Beef Tub slope

LANDSCAPE Dramatic Beef Tub hollow and views of the Borderlands

SUGGESTED MAP OS Explorer 330 Moffat & St Mary's Loch

START/FINISH Grid reference: NT 057128

DOG FRIENDLINESS Keep on lead when passing sheep and cattle

PARKING Lay-by just south of forest gateway

PUBLIC TOILETS Lay-by just south of forest gateway

WARNING Bull with cows occasionally at Point ④

Dark, forbidding and dramatic (Sir Walter Scott once described it as a 'black, blackguard-looking abyss of a hole'), the hollow known as the Devil's Beef Tub has a history as turbulent as its name suggests. Over the years this deep, natural bowl has been used as a hiding place by thieves, formed a refuge for the persecuted and witnessed feats of daring – and even murder. Once known as the Corrie of Annan, it gained the name the Devil's Beef Tub in the 16th century when it was frequently used by the Johnstone clan, a local reiving (rustling) family, to hide stolen cattle after a raid. In reference to this it was also sometimes sardonically referred to as the Marquis of Annandale's Beef Stand.

The Covenanting Movement

The Tub was not only useful for sheltering stolen animals, however – it was also used as a hideout by persecuted Covenanters during Charles II's so-called 'Killing Times'. The origins of the covenanting movement went back to the time when bishops were imposed on the Church of Scotland by James VI. Years later his son, Charles I, who also believed in the divine right of kings, tried to interfere further in Scottish ecclesiastical affairs. This provoked such hostility that there was a riot in Edinburgh, resulting in the signing of the National Covenant in 1638. This document affirmed the authority of the Church of Scotland over the King in all spiritual matters and was circulated throughout Scotland, gaining particular support among Scots in the south-west.

Throughout the 17th century, religious fanaticism grew and Covenanters became a powerful force in Scotland. When Charles II, who had Roman Catholic sympathies, was restored to the throne he tried to suppress the movement. There were many battles and prisoners were often brutally treated. Finding themselves outlawed, some ministers of the Church began holding illegal services, known as 'conventicles', in the open air. Persecution only fuelled resistance and during the years 1684 to 1687, the 'Killing Times', hundreds of people were slaughtered by officers of the

DEVIL'S BEEF TUB

Crown. The most notorious of these was Graham of Claverhouse, later Viscount Dundee. There's a reminder of these violent times near the car park at the Devil's Beef Tub, where you can see a stone dedicated to John Hunter, a Covenanter who was shot on the hills here in 1685.

A Rebel in the Tub

This violent period in history came to an end when James II's son-in-law, William of Orange, came to the throne in 1689 – but was soon replaced in the following century by the violence of the Jacobite rebellion. In 1746 a prisoner from the Battle of Culloden, which had brought the rebellion to an end the previous year, was being marched to Carlisle for trial.

He escaped his guards by leaping into the Devil's Beef Tub and disappearing in the swirling mist. Once again this great hollow had played its part in Scottish history.

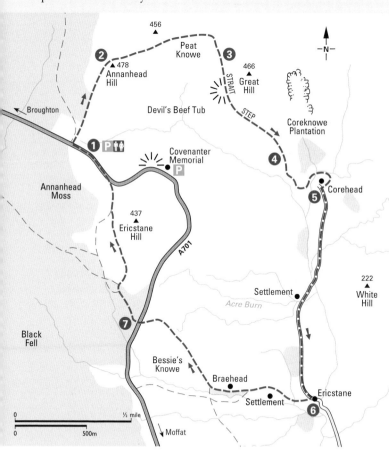

WALK 1 DIRECTIONS

1 Walk up the A701 to the forest gateway on the right. Don't take the wide gravel track, but a wooden gate on the right-hand side, to a small path to the left of a fence. Climb rails at a fence end, and head up the grassy slope of Annanhead Hill, keeping to the right of the plantation area to the trig point on the summit.

2 The small path continues around the flank of Peat Knowe, keeping the wall and fence to your left. Follow the path down the grassy slope of Annanhead Hill, keeping to the head of a gully, where your path meets the wall. Walk to the other side of the gully.

WHERE TO EAT AND DRINK
The Balmoral Hotel and the Ariffe Café on the main square in Moffat are both excellent choices. If you've got a sweet tooth there's always the delights of the Moffat Toffee Shop.

WHILE YOU'RE THERE
Moffat has several historical associations. Robert Burns wrote one of his poems at the Black Bull Hotel and Graham of Claverhouse, the scourge of the Covenanters, once stayed here. Of more recent interest is the fact that the town was the birthplace of Air Chief Marshal Lord Dowding, who led Fighter Command in the Battle of Britain.

3 Past the gully head, turn right on a small path that runs just above, and to the left of, the grassy gully. As the slope drops away steeply, the path, called Strait Step, bends left and contours on a level line across the steep slope, below some small craggy outcrops. As the slope eases, the path slants down through bracken, heading towards the Coreknowe plantation at the valley end. Just before the plantation, you'll reach a metal gate leading into a field.

4 A bull occasionally grazes in this field, so if you need to avoid him, pass along above the field and climb an awkward fence into the plantation. Slant down right, under the trees, to a gate into the field with the tiny footbridge

WHAT TO LOOK OUT FOR
Ericstane Hill, which you pass on the latter part of this walk, was the site of a Roman signal station, used to monitor troop movements along a Roman road that stretched all the way from Carlisle to the Clyde.

mentioned below. Otherwise, go through the grey gate and down beside a grassy bank. Turn left on a rough track to the bottom corner of the plantation. The track reaches a gate above a red-brick house. Through the gate, signed 'Moffat', head out into the field to a tiny footbridge, then bear right to pass to the left of the white buildings of Corehead farm. A fence on the right leads to a gate on to the farm's access track.

5 Follow the farm road along the valley bottom. The small area of undulating land on the right is the remains of an ancient settlement.

6 After a cattle grid, at the start of the buildings, turn up right through a gate signed 'footpath'. A stony track leads past a house and through a gate. Turn right, following the track as it runs above a stone wall. Eventually you'll reach the main A701. Cross over – take care as it's busy – on to a rough track opposite.

7 The route passes over Ericstane Hill. Bear right and follow the track as it runs north round the far side of the hill. On open hill, the track is indistinct, deep ruts half-hidden under rushes. Pass through a slight col to the left of the hill summit, to rejoin the A701. Turn right here to visit the Covenanter memorial, or turn left to return to the start of the walk.

Going the Whole Hogg in Ettrick

An enjoyable tramp in the footsteps of a local poet.

DISTANCE 7 miles (11.3km)	**MINIMUM TIME** 4hrs
ASCENT/GRADIENT 420ft (128m) ▲▲▲	**LEVEL OF DIFFICULTY** +++

PATHS Hill tracks and grassy paths; pathless grass for Peniestone Knowe loop; 2 stiles

LANDSCAPE Open rolling hills and loch side

SUGGESTED MAP OS Explorer 330 Moffat & St Mary's Loch

START/FINISH Grid reference: NT 2237204

DOG FRIENDLINESS Keep on lead near sheep

PARKING On both sides of A708 near Glen Café

PUBLIC TOILETS At start behind Glen Café

James Hogg, a shepherd turned writer, was born in this tranquil valley in 1770. He and his beloved dog frequently paced tracks that you follow on this walk, from Ettrick to Tibbie Shiels Inn, to meet Sir Walter Scott.

Hogg is popularly known as the Ettrick Shepherd and a monument to him broods above the start of this walk. However, he would probably prefer to be remembered by his work, as his literary achievements are considerable – particularly for someone who had such humble origins. The son of a poor farmer, he hardly received any formal education – indeed, some reports state that his schooling lasted no more than six months. By the age of seven he had started work as a cowherd on a farm.

But he had ambition and determination, and an artistic streak, perhaps inherited from his grandfather, said to be the last man who could speak to the fairies. By the time Hogg reached his mid-teens he was working as a shepherd and had taught himself to read and write. He began composing poetry while out on the hills, drawing on the tradition of local ballads learned from his mother. He soon came to the attention of Sir Walter Scott, who was travelling the Borders. Scott became Hogg's mentor – although the pronounced differences in their class meant that Scott always regarded him as a bit of a peasant.

Hogg modelled himself on Robert Burns and began to get his poems and songs published. His first collection of ballads, *The Mountain Bard* (1807) was well received, and three years later Hogg moved to Edinburgh to try and make it as a writer. Within a few years he had been recognised as one of the leading poets of the day – the poor country shepherd had now become a celebrity.

After a few years Hogg returned to the Borders, where he wrote the work for which he is best remembered – *The Private Memoirs and Confessions of a Justified Sinner* (1824). Contemporary critics felt it was so sophisticated that it could never have been written by such an uneducated man. James Hogg was eventually offered a knighthood, but his wife made him turn it down. He died in 1835 and is buried in Ettrick churchyard.

Selkirk ↑

St Mary's Loch

▲ 427

James Hogg Statue
● Tibbie Shiels Inn

SOUTHERN

—N—

A708

Loch o the Lowes

▲ 518

▲ 377
Riskinhope Rig

UPLAND

▲ 378

Crosscleuch Burn

WAY

▲ 394

6

Riskinhope House ●

▲ 446

Little Yarrow

▲ 461
Peat Hill

Riskinhope Hope ●

5

▲ 466

Moffat,
Grey Mare's Tail

WAY

Riskinhope Burn

Whithope Burn

▲ 531

Pikestone Rig

3

UPLAND

0   ½ mile

0   500m

Peniestone Knowe
▲ 551

4

SOUTHERN

WALK 2 DIRECTIONS

1 Take the lane across the stone bridge between the two lochs and past Tibbie Shiels Inn, then take the rougher track uphill through

a gate, with the Crosscleuch Burn down on its right. It winds uphill to a gate into plantations.

2 At once, fork right, at a Southern Upland Way (SUW)

signpost. The path crosses a footbridge, then runs up a tree gap past a signpost, to a stile at the plantation edge. It descends to a footbridge over Whithope Burn, then heads up valley past the ruins of Riskinhope Hope among scattered trees. It then turns uphill, with plenty of waymarkers, to the level ridgeline of Pikestone Rig. Head along the ridge for 550yds (500m) to reach a small col. Here the SUW bears left, on to the ridge flank; meanwhile another path turns sharp back right out of the col. Later, this will be the descent for Riskinhope.

❸ Ignoring both those paths, keep ahead up the grassy ridgeline, on a quad-bike track. Peniestone Knowe's plateau is rough and pathless. The actual summit is marked by a pool, and a slight knoll where three fences and a fallen wall all meet.

❹ Don't cross any fence, but follow the fence running downhill to the left. Quad-bike wheelmarks run down fairly steep ground with rushes, to a stile where the SUW crosses the fence. Turn sharp left, away from the stile, and follow the wide, rebuilt path along the flank of Peniestone Knowe to the col on Pikestone Rig (Point ❸). Go slantwise through the col, on

to the path already noted, which slants down the left flank of the ridge. On the left is the notch of Riskinhope Burn and the path runs down along the right wall of this. It is grassy but clear, until it passes below a wide col before Peat Hill. Here it vanishes in a boggy patch, for just a few steps, before reappearing on the bracken slope of Peat Hill.

❺ The grassy track slants down the flank of Peat Hill, then zig-zags down through two gates to the valley floor meadow. Before Riskinhope house it reaches a ford of Riskinhope Burn. Now follow the burn down to reach the Loch of the Lowes.

❻ Turn right along the loch side. Go through a gate above the loch's corner, to a bracken path. This continues alongside the loch to a gate at its northern corner. Bear left to a high footbridge. Cross a field near the river to a gate on to the lane beside the bridge between the lochs and back to your car.

A Poet's Passions at Langholm

An exhilarating climb is followed by a more gentle stroll past Hugh MacDiarmid's memorial.

DISTANCE 3.75 miles (6km) **MINIMUM TIME** 2hrs

ASCENT/GRADIENT 919ft (280m) ▲▲▲ **LEVEL OF DIFFICULTY** ✚✚✚

PATHS Firm hill paths and tarmac roads

LANDSCAPE Lush green borderlands and fine views

SUGGESTED MAP OS Explorer 323 Eskdale & Castle O'er Forest

START/FINISH Grid reference: NY 364849

DOG FRIENDLINESS Keep on lead as there are plenty of sheep

PARKING Riverside car park (free)

PUBLIC TOILETS At car park and off main street of Langholm

The Scots have long been passionate about their independence and take great pride in their rich culture. On this walk you'll pass a memorial to one of the founding fathers of the modern Scottish nationalist movement – the poet Hugh MacDiarmid.

A Cultural Giant

MacDiarmid, whose real name was Christopher Murray Grieve, was born in Langholm in 1892 and is considered one of Scotland's leading 20th-century poets. His early working life was spent in journalism, working in Montrose and London, and he then turned to writing poetry. A man of passionate views – he was a communist and nationalist – his verses were written in local dialect, mixed with words taken from the older Scottish tongue. His volumes of poetry included *Sangschaw*, his first book which was published in 1925, *Penny Wheep* (1926) and *A Drunk Man Looks at the Thistle* (1926). His works sparked a renewed interest in Scottish language and culture and he became a central figure in the country's literary revival.

Championing Home Rule

During the 1930s he moved to Shetland, where he continued to write. He made a great impression on those who met him there and was once described as: 'Unmistakably the genius, with tensely thoughtful features and smouldering, deep-set eyes... [he is] almost rustically Scots... wearing a kilt and a plaid, both of bright tartan.' Years later another writer was to describe him as 'a magnificent mouse of a man'. He was by this time involved in the early nationalist movement, which had started in Scotland after the First World War and grew in strength during the 1920s. Together with other writers, such as Lewis Spence and Neil Gunn, MacDiarmid voiced a desire for Home Rule for Scotland. The movement grew into the Scottish National Party which was formed in 1934.

After the Second World War, MacDiarmid moved back to the Borders, living with his wife in a two-room labourer's cottage near Biggar. It was simple in the extreme and had no water or electricity, but it was from here that he embarked on lecture tours all over the world.

MacDiarmid died in 1978 and was buried in Langholm, against the wishes of the local 'gentry' who disliked his radical views. Above the door of his old home are inscribed the telling words:

> *The rose of all the world is not for me*
> *I want for my part*
> *Only the little white rose of Scotland*
> *That smells sharp and sweet and breaks the heart*

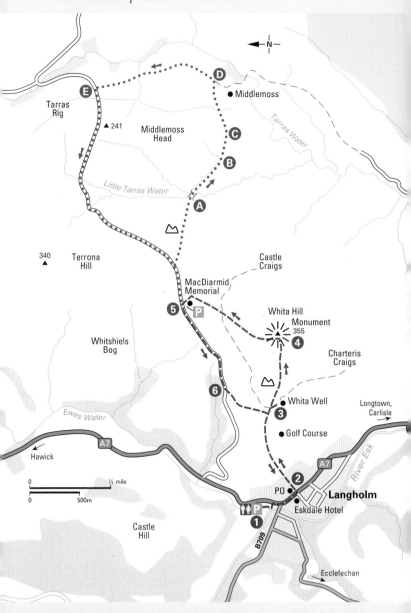

Overleaf: Memorial to Hugh MacDiarmid on a hill at Langholm (Walk 3)

WALK

3

WALK 3 DIRECTIONS

1 Cross grass downstream, then go through a hedge gap on the left to pass through a small garden to the A7 above. Head into Langholm along the High Street to the post office on the left.

2 Immediately past the post office, turn left up Kirk Wynd. It becomes a tarred path, then a rough track running up to the left of the golf course to a gate. Follow the grassy path up and slightly right to reach a green seat beside Whita Well, a natural spring.

3 Now take the path to the left of the seat, running steeply up the hill. Follow it under a line of pylons and up to the top of Whita Hill. There are stone steps up to the monument, a 100ft (30m) high obelisk commemorating Sir John Malcolm, a famous soldier, diplomat and scholar.

4 From Sir John Malcolm's monument, walk back a few paces to join the wide gravel track that runs in front of it, then turn right. It's easy walking now, following this clear track downhill. Eventually you'll reach a metal sculpture on the left-hand side. The sculpture, which resembles an open book, was created by Jake Harvey as a memorial to the poet Hugh MacDiarmid.

5 Bear left past the sculpture to a small car park, and turn left. You now simply follow the road as it winds downhill – it's quite a long stretch but it's fairly quiet. Go back under the line of pylons then, just after a copse on your right-hand side, take the path found on the left, signposted 'Langholm Walks 10'.

6 Follow this footpath, slightly uphill and then above a wall, where it runs through a small boggy patch. After this you shortly return to the gate you reached on your outward journey. Turn right, through the gate, and retrace your outward route.

And on Across the Moors

A loop that takes you to a remote farm.
See map and information panel for Walk 3

DISTANCE 3.5 miles (5.7km)   **MINIMUM TIME** 1hr 30min
ASCENT/GRADIENT 427ft (130m) ▲▲▲   **LEVEL OF DIFFICULTY** ✦✦✦

WALK 4 DIRECTIONS
(Walk 3 option)

From Point ❺ on the main walk, turn right and walk over the cattle grid. After about 100yds (91m) turn to your right, away from the road, and follow the narrow path that plunges steeply down the hill, running parallel with a wall far off to the right. There's lots of bracken covering the slopes.

Eventually you'll come down to a burn. Follow the path across the footbridge and continue uphill with a small stream trickling to your left. On the crest of the hill (Point ❸) continue in the same direction to reach a wall (Point ❹). Turn left now and follow the wall until you pass a house on the right-hand side. Follow the path through two gates, passing an entrance to the farm on your right. The path can be rather muddy here, but keep walking to another gate where you join a wide firm track (Point ❹).

You now turn left, following the track past a line of telegraph poles on the left-hand side – there are sheep here, so watch your dog. You'll eventually go over a small bridge and will come on to the main road (Point ❺).

Turn left and walk along the road. Traffic does come along here but it is generally fairly quiet.

On the right-hand side are areas where peat is cut for use by local people as fuel. The road starts to climb uphill and you'll eventually come back to the MacDiarmid monument where you rejoin the main walk at Point ❺.

WHAT TO LOOK FOR

Take a look at the Town Head Bridge in Langholm. Thomas Telford (1757–1834) was involved in its construction when he was a journeyman. He was born in Dumfriesshire, the son of a local shepherd who died when Thomas was only three months old. Telford served an apprenticeship as a stonemason in Langholm and trained himself to be an architect. He moved on to Edinburgh in order to work on the building of the New Town, and later went to London. Telford, who is one of Scotland's greatest engineers, is most famous as a bridge builder, but he also carried out many road surveys. This gave him the nickname 'Colossus of Roads'. It was he who surveyed the Carlisle–Glasgow road – one of the motorways of its day. He is buried in Westminster Abbey.

From Selkirk to the Wilds of Africa

A gentle walk by Ettrick Water, laced with memories of the great explorer Mungo Park.

DISTANCE 4 miles (6.4km)	**MINIMUM TIME** 1hr 40min
ASCENT/GRADIENT 131ft (40m) ▲▲▲	**LEVEL OF DIFFICULTY** ✦✦✦

PATHS Riverside paths and woodland tracks, town streets, 4 stiles
LANDSCAPE Undulating farmland and dense woodland
SUGGESTED MAP OS Explorer 338 Galashiels, Selkirk & Montrose
START/FINISH Grid reference: NT 469286
DOG FRIENDLINESS Good, but don't let them chase ducks
PARKING West Port car park in Selkirk
PUBLIC TOILETS At car park

WALK 5 DIRECTIONS

It's hard to imagine that sleepy Selkirk has any connection with the wilds of Africa. But look carefully at the statue in the High Street and you'll see that it commemorates Mungo Park, a local man and noted explorer. Park, born in 1771, trained as a doctor but, instead of settling down to a comfortable life, he took a post as surgeon's mate on a ship bound for the East Indies. This gave him a taste for travel and, on returning from the voyage, he promptly set off again, this time heading for Africa to map the Niger. He returned safely to Scotland after an eventful journey and wrote a fascinating account of his adventures called *Travels in the Interior Districts of Africa*. However, his taste for adventure was not yet sated but he was not so lucky on his next adventure, drowning in the turbulent waters of the Niger while trying to escape from hostile tribesmen.

Start at Park's statue and go right down Ettrick Terrace, left at the church, then immediately sharp right down Forest Road. Follow this downhill, cutting off the corner using the steps after No 109, to Mill Street. Go right, then left on to Buccleuch Road. Turn right following the signs for the riverside walk and continue to walk across Victoria Park to join a tarmac track.

WHILE YOU'RE THERE

Bowhill, home of the Duke and Duchess of Buccleuch and Queensberry, is 3 miles (4.8km) west of Selkirk on the A708. This fine Georgian house is stuffed full of art treasures, with paintings by Canaletto, Reynolds, Van Dyck and Gainsborough, as well as elegant furniture, silver and porcelain. It's a good place to bring children as they've also got a restored Victorian kitchen and a country park with an adventure area and nature trails.

Turn left, walk by the river, then join the road and turn right to cross the bridge. Turn left along Ettrickhaugh Road, passing a row of cottages on your left. Just past the cottages, turn left

and cross a tiny footbridge. Then turn left down some steps and follow the path to the river bank and turn right.

Follow the path along the river margin; it's eroded in places so watch your step. In spring and summer your way is sprinkled with delicate wild flowers. Eventually you join a wider track and bear left. Follow this until you reach a weir and a salmon ladder. Turn right to cross the tiny bridge.

Immediately after this go left and continue walking alongside the river until you reach a point at which the Yarrow Water joins the Ettrick Water. Retrace your steps for about 100yds (91m), then turn left at a crossing of tracks.

Your route now takes you through the woods, until you cross over the little bridge by the weir again. Take the footpath to the left and follow the cinder/gravel track round the meadow until you come to the mill buildings.

Bear right (but don't cross the bridge) and continue, walking with the mill lade (small canal) on your left. Where the path splits, take the track on the left to follow a straight, concrete path beside the water to reach an abandoned fish farm.

Walk around the buildings, then bear left to continue following the mill lade. Go left over the footbridge, then right, passing the cottages again. At the main road go right to reach the bridge. Don't cross the bridge but join the footpath on the left.

WHERE TO EAT AND DRINK

There are a few places that you can try in the centre of Selkirk. Among the hotels offering a range of bar meals is the Cross Keys by the Market Place, which serves toasted sandwiches and light snacks. There's also a small tea room. Look out for the famous Selkirk bannock – a type of fruit bread – on sale in the town bakeries.

Follow this footpath as it goes past a sports ground, then skirts a housing estate. Continue walking until you reach the pedestrian footbridge on your right-hand side, where you cross over the river, bear right, then retrace your footsteps back over Victoria Park and uphill to the Market Place at the start of the walk.

WHAT TO LOOK OUT FOR

You've got a great chance of seeing a dipper on this walk, particularly around the river banks at the point where the Ettrick Water and the Yarrow Water meet. Also sometimes known as the water ouzel, it is a pretty little brown bird with a white breast. It feeds on insects, often wading through rushing water and bobbing up and down while searching for them – hence its name.

Remembering the Reivers at Newcastleton

A quiet walk through borderlands where cattle raiding was once a part of everyday life for the local inhabitants.

DISTANCE 5.75 miles (9.2km)   MINIMUM TIME 2hrs 45min

ASCENT/GRADIENT 689ft (210m) ▲▲▲   LEVEL OF DIFFICULTY ✦✦✦

PATHS Quiet byroads and farm tracks, one grassy climb

LANDSCAPE Rolling borderlands and moors

SUGGESTED MAP OS Explorer 324 Liddesdale & Kershope Forest

START/FINISH Grid reference: NY 483875

DOG FRIENDLINESS Dogs on lead; sheep, cows and ponies graze on route

PARKING Douglas Square

PUBLIC TOILETS Langholm Street, next to fire station

It might seem quiet today, but the area around Newcastleton was once what tabloid newspapers would now describe as 'war-torn'. Ownership of these borderlands was hotly disputed between England and Scotland for hundreds of years and there were frequent battles and skirmishes. You'll pass a reminder of those turbulent days on this walk.

Raids and Revenge

Because places like Newcastleton were so remote from the centres of power in both London and Edinburgh, they were difficult to defend and had a reputation for lawlessness. Feuds often developed between powerful local families, and violent raids and cases of cattle rustling (reiving) were common – cattle were a valuable asset. These were ruthless people who could probably have shown the Vikings a thing or two.

A raid would commonly be followed by an illegal revenge attack (which of course was better fun, being illegal) or sometimes a legal 'Hot Trod'. This was a pursuit mounted immediately after a raid and had strict rules – including one stating that a lighted turf had to be carried if the trod crossed the border. When reivers were caught they were often taken hostage (the ransom money was very handy), taken prisoner, or even killed. Not surprisingly the countryside became studded with sturdy castles and fortified 'pele' towers, so that people could better defend themselves.

The most powerful family in this area were the Armstrongs, the principal reiving clan in the Borders. They were extremely influential and held large tracts of land. Their main seat was Mangerton Tower, the rather pitiful remains of which you can see on this walk. The Armstrongs were said to be able to muster 3,000 mounted men whenever they wished to launch a raid into England. They were ruthless and violent, running a rather successful protection racket as one of their money-making ventures. Imagine the mafia with cows and you'll get the picture.

It wasn't until the Union of the Crowns took place in 1603, following the death of Queen Elizabeth I, that the Border wars ceased and the power of the reiving clans was finally dispersed. Keen to gain control and make his mark as an effective ruler of the new united kingdom, James VI of Scotland (James I of England) banned weapons and established mounted forces to police the area. Reiving families – often identified with the help of local informers – were scattered and members transported or even executed.

After Archibald Armstrong of Mangerton was executed in 1610, the Armstrongs lost their lands to the Scotts, another powerful local family. However, the family didn't disappear and members of this once fearsome tribe have continued to make their mark on the world. Most famous of all must be Neil Armstrong, who carried a fragment of Armstrong tartan when he stepped on to the surface of the moon, in 1969.

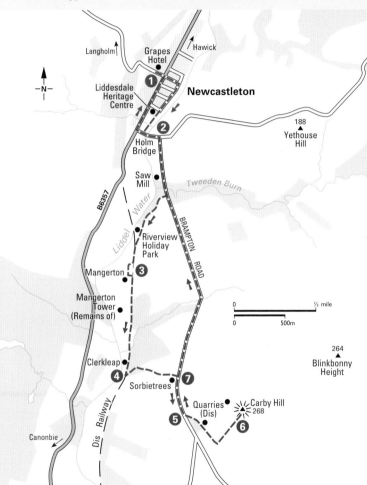

WALK 6 DIRECTIONS

❶ From Douglas Square in the centre of Newcastleton, with your back to the Grapes Hotel, walk along Whitchester Street (or any of the other streets opposite) and go down to the river, the Liddel Water. Turn right, then walk along the river bank and join the footpath downstream to reach Holm Bridge. Here, turn left at the top of the steps and then cross over the bridge.

WALK 6

❷ After about 100yds (91m), turn right and follow the Brampton Road, passing static caravans on either side. You'll eventually pass an old saw mill with a corrugated iron roof and will then reach the Tweeden Burn Bridge. Cross the bridge and walk uphill, then turn right and join the metalled track signed for Riverview Holiday Park. Continue on this road until you near the farm buildings.

❸ At the farm entrance, fork left on to the bed of the old railway line, which has joined you from the right. This line once linked Carlisle to Edinburgh but was closed following the Beeching cuts of 1963. Follow the line as it leads past the remains of Mangerton Tower, in a field to your right, and continue ahead until you reach Clerkleap cottage.

❹ Walk 50yds (45m) beyond the cottage and turn left over a

rotting gate. A rough path leads up left then turns right to join a rough track. This leads through woodland and on, uphill, to join the road by Sorbietrees farm. Turn right now and walk along the road, past the farm, to a small stand of conifers on the left. Turn left through the gate.

❺ Bear right now and head up the left-hand side of the trees. Walk past the top of the wood following a dry-stone wall up below a former quarry to the field's top corner. Climb over the field gate ahead. Now open grassy slopes lead up left, to the cairn and fallen walls on the summit of Carby Hill. The views are truly great from here. Known locally as Caerba Hill, this was the site of a prehistoric settlement.

❻ Retrace your steps to reach the road again, then turn right and walk back past Sorbietrees farm.

❼ At the farm, continue on the main road as it bears right and follow it back over the Tweeden Burn Bridge and up to the Holm Bridge. Cross the bridge and walk straight on for 100yds (91m), then turn right on to the B6357 and walk back to the village square via the little heritage centre.

Thirty-Nine Steps in Broughton

*A lovely walk through landscapes
immortalised by John Buchan.*

DISTANCE 5 miles (8km)	**MINIMUM TIME** 2hrs 30min
ASCENT/GRADIENT 1,575ft (480m) ▲▲▲	**LEVEL OF DIFFICULTY** +++

PATHS Hill tracks and grassy paths, 1 stile

LANDSCAPE Rolling hills and exposed ridge

SUGGESTED MAP OS Explorer 336 Biggar & Broughton

START/FINISH Grid reference: NT 119374

DOG FRIENDLINESS Good, but keep on lead because of sheep

PARKING Parking in front of cottage past Broughton Place and art gallery

PUBLIC TOILETS None en route

> *I had been walking for about half an hour when I spotted a man
> standing alone on Broughton Heights. I thought nothing of it
> until he began to wave urgently. Thinking he was in some sort
> of trouble I climbed the hill. When I reached the top I saw that
> he was dressed in a tweed jacket and carried a small pack. His
> piercing blue eyes met mine: 'Hello Hannay,' he said holding out
> his hand. 'I have a message for you. We need your help.'*

John Buchan didn't write those words, but these rugged hills around
Broughton were once familiar and often trodden by the author of
The Thirty-Nine Steps and you can't help but be inspired to flights of fancy
by memories of his taut tales of intrigue and derring-do. Although he
was born in Perth (in 1875), Buchan has close links with this area as his
grandparents lived here and he spent many summer holidays in the village.
A keen hillwalker, it is almost certain that he followed the same tracks that
you take on this exhilarating circuit.

'Shockers'

Buchan's most famous fictional creation is the upper-class hero Richard
Hannay, who featured in the spy thriller *The Thirty-Nine Steps* (1915).
But this was not his only novel. He wrote many other adventure stories
(or 'shockers' as he liked to call them) – four of them featuring Richard
Hannay, as well as a book of poetry and several historical works including
biographies of Sir Walter Scott and Oliver Cromwell.

A Career to Envy

He was extraordinarily successful and must have greatly annoyed his
contemporaries who could never have hoped to match his achievements.
After Oxford University (where he naturally became President of
the Union and gained a First), he became a barrister. During the First
World War he was appointed Director of Information, and then wrote a
24-volume history of the war. In 1927 he became a Member of Parliament

and was made a Companion of Honour in 1932 – publishing more works all the time. As his career flourished he came into contact with many great characters, including Henry James and Lawrence of Arabia.

Buchan must have had immense energy and obviously impressed those around him, for in 1935 he was appointed Governor-General of Canada and was given a peerage – taking the title Baron Tweedsmuir of Elsfield. Tweedsmuir is a hamlet close to the village of Broughton and the area featured in a number of Buchan's works. Broughton was the village of 'Woodilee' in a little-known novel *Witch Wood* (1927), while much of the action in his adventure novels is played out on the moody moors and lonely hills of the Borders. John Buchan died in Canada in 1940. He would probably be surprised to find that his 'shockers' are still being read and enjoyed today.

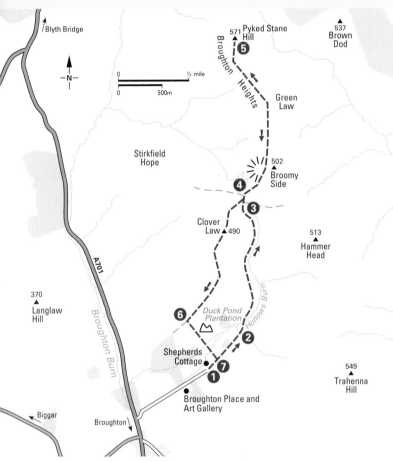

WALK 7 DIRECTIONS

❶ From the parking place, go through the gate and follow the obvious, grassy track that runs in front of the cottage. You'll soon pass a copse on the left-hand side, then pass the attractively named Duck Pond Plantation, also on the left-hand side. The track becomes slightly rougher now, and you cross a small footbridge over a burn.

BROUGHTON

2 Your track continues ahead past feathery carpets of heather and bracken – listen for the skylarks in the summer. Continue walking and the path will soon level out and lead you past a gully on the right-hand side. Follow the track until it bends, after which you come to a meeting of tracks.

3 Take the track that bears left and head for the dip that lies between the two hills – Clover Law on the left and Broomy Side in front. You should just be able to spot the fence 100yds (91m) on the skyline. Make for that fence and, as you near it, you'll eventually spot a gate, next to which is a wooden stile.

WHILE YOU'RE THERE

If you're a real John Buchan fan you can make a pilgrimage to the John Buchan Centre, which is at the far end of Broughton village. It's housed in an old church where Buchan and his relatives once attended services. This small museum is full of photographs, books and general memorabilia that illustrate the life and achievements of the author and politician.

4 Cross the stile, then turn right and follow the fence line. You soon get superb views to the left – well, you do on a clear day. Continue following the fence and walk up the track until you reach the trig point on Broughton Heights – the final ascent's a bit of a puff – but it's thankfully not too long.

WHERE TO EAT AND DRINK

The best place for tea is the Laurel Bank tea room, which can be found in the centre of Broughton. It serves home-made soup and light meals such as baked potatoes and toasted sandwiches, substantial meals such as mince and tatties, as well as freshly baked cakes and scones. The atmosphere is friendly and they're used to accommodating walkers.

5 Now retrace your steps to reach the stile again, nip over it, but this time turn right and follow the narrow track that climbs Clover Law. Continue walking in the same direction, following the fence line as it runs along the top of the ridge. When you near the end of the ridge, keep your eyes peeled for a path to the left, down an old earth boundary bank.

6 Follow the track as it runs down roughly in the direction of the cottage – it's quite a steep descent. At the bottom you'll come to an old wall and a burn, which you cross, then continue ahead to cross over another burn and across a field to reach the main track.

7 Turn right here and walk past the little cottage again, through the gate and back to your car. If you want to visit Broughton Place and its art gallery, just continue walking down the track to reach the house on your left.

WHAT TO LOOK OUT FOR

The Broughton Gallery showcases the work of leading British artists and craftspeople. As well as paintings in oil and watercolour, you can find hand-made glass, ceramics, painted silk, carved wood and distinctive jewellery. The goods are for sale so you'd better bring your credit card – you might find a local landscape that you just can't resist.

A Reference to Peebles

*There are reminders of the founders
of an encyclopaedia on this lovely walk.*

WALK 8

DISTANCE *3.5 miles (5.7km)*   **MINIMUM TIME** *1hr 20min*

ASCENT/GRADIENT *295ft (90m)* ▲▲▲   **LEVEL OF DIFFICULTY** +++

PATHS *Waymarked riverside paths and metalled tracks*

LANDSCAPE *Rolling borderlands and Tweed Valley*

SUGGESTED MAP *OS Explorer 337 Peebles & Innerleithen*

START/FINISH *Grid reference: NT 250402*

DOG FRIENDLINESS *Great, chance to swim in the river*

PARKING *Kingsmeadows Road car park, Peebles*

PUBLIC TOILETS *At car park*

Next time you're watching *University Challenge*, listening to *Brain of Britain*, or even taking part in your local pub quiz night, think for a moment about the person who has compiled the questions. They've almost certainly come up with some of them after referring to an encyclopaedia. We tend to take these great tomes for granted, assuming that everything they say is correct, giving little thought to the people that produce them. This walk starts and finishes in Peebles – the birthplace of the Chambers brothers, the founding publishers of the famous *Chambers' Encyclopaedia*.

William, the older brother, was born in 1800 and in 1814 was apprenticed to a bookseller in Edinburgh. Robert, born in 1802, later followed him to the city and in 1819 they set up in business as booksellers, then branched out into printing as well. They seemed to have a flair for the trade and, in 1832, William started *Chambers' Edinburgh Journal,* a publication to which Robert contributed many essays. It was a success and later that year the brothers established the publishing house W & R Chambers. Robert, who seemed to be the more literary of the two, continued to write in his spare time and in 1844 anonymously published a book with the less-than-catchy title *Vestiges of the Natural History of Creation*. It was a controversial work, dealing with issues that were then considered blasphemy. Charles Darwin later praised it, saying it had helped to prepare the ground for his book *On the Origin of Species* (1859).

An Encyclopaedia is Born

The first edition of the *Chambers' Encyclopaedia* (1859–68) encompassed ten volumes and was edited by Robert. It was based on a translation of a German work. Robert, who had become friendly with Sir Walter Scott, continued to write, producing books on a wide range of subjects such as history, literature and geology. He also wrote a reference work entitled *A Biographical Dictionary of Eminent Scotsmen* (1832–4).

Although not as prolific as his brother, William too wrote a number of books, including a *History of Peeblesshire*, which came out in 1864. He did not forget his origins in Peebles and in 1859 he founded and endowed a museum, library and art gallery in the town. It's still there today, on the High Street, and is worth visiting, if only for an enormous frieze – a copy of the Elgin marbles that were taken from the Parthenon in Athens. When the brothers died, Robert in 1871 and William in 1883, the company was taken over by Robert's son. The name Chambers is still associated with scholarly reference works today.

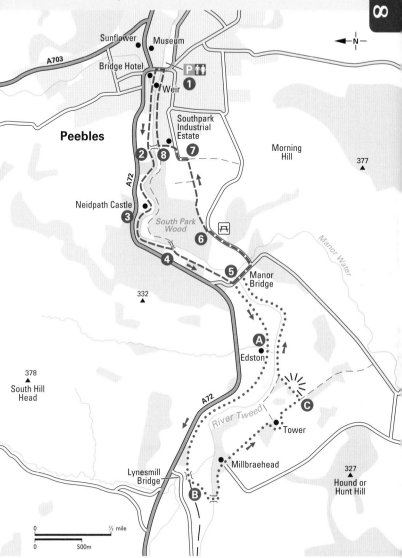

WALK 8 DIRECTIONS

❶ From Kingsmeadows car park, turn right and cross the bridge. Turn left at the Bridge Hotel and walk down the slope,

past the swimming pool, to the river. Cross a small footbridge, go up some steps, turn left, descend some steps and follow the riverside track to pass a metal bridge and a children's play area.

WALK

8

2 Continue following the obvious path and go over a little bridge over a burn, after which the path becomes a little more rugged. You now enter the woods, going through a gate. Eventually you'll leave the woods and will come to the medieval, romantic-looking Neidpath Castle on the right-hand side.

3 From the castle continue walking by the river to go through another gate. You'll soon come on to higher ground and will get a great view of the old railway bridge spanning the water in front of you. After another kissing gate, maintain your direction to reach the red sandstone bridge.

4 Go up to the right of the bridge, so that you join the old railway line – you now maintain direction and continue following the Tweed Walk. Follow along this disused track until you find yourself at another attractive bridge – Manor Bridge.

WHILE YOU'RE THERE

Neidpath Castle dates back to the 14th century. Its walls are 11ft (3m) thick and conceal a pit prison as well as several historic rooms. It never really saw much action, except for the time in 1650 when it found itself besieged by Cromwell and his forces.

5 Turn left here and cross the bridge, then take the turning on the left signed 'Tweed Walk'. You're now on a quiet lane that winds uphill – do stop and look behind you for classic views of the Borders landscape, with lush rolling hills and the wide, busy Tweed. Continue until you reach a track on the left that leads into the woods, opposite a picnic site.

WHERE TO EAT AND DRINK

There are plenty of places to choose from in Peebles. The Sunflower is a contemporary restaurant just off the main street. You can get cappuccino and a large piece of cake or choose one of their delicious and well-presented main meals.

6 Follow this path uphill, parallel to the road. Just before the path rejoins the road, continue down a wide, grassy path signposted to Peebles, with woodland to the left. Beyond a gate, the path runs through fields until you join a tarmac road.

7 Follow this road and turn left beyond the Southpark Garage into Southpark Industrial Estate, following signs to Riverside Path. Walk between the units. Go down some steps and bear left when you reach the bottom. You'll soon reach a footbridge ahead of you.

8 Turn right here and follow the wide track beside the river. This is a popular part of the walk and attracts lots of families on sunny days. Continue walking past the weir, then go up the steps at the bridge and cross over to return to the car park.

And a Note on the Tweed

A longer walk along the banks of the Tweed.
See map and information panel for Walk 8

DISTANCE *3.5 miles (5.7km)* **MINIMUM TIME** *1hr 30min*
ASCENT/GRADIENT *66ft (20m)* ▲▲▲ **LEVEL OF DIFFICULTY** ✦✦✦

WALK 9 DIRECTIONS
(Walk 8 option)

At Point ❺ on the walk, don't turn left across the bridge but simply cross to the other side, nip over the stile and go up some steps to rejoin the old railway line. It's easy going and you just follow the path which is laced with hawthorn, birch and willow trees, as well as brambles, nettles, wild roses and gorse. Eventually you'll pass Edston farm (Point Ⓐ) on the right-hand side and might have to cross a couple of stiles on the track (if the gates aren't opened).

The track now takes you further from the river and is full of wild flowers in the spring and summer. Cross another couple of stiles and follow the track as it narrows, then eventually opens out into pasture. You'll pass a small house over to the right and will then see lovely old Lynesmill Bridge, also on the right.

Your route now takes you over an old railway bridge. Turn left at the end (Point Ⓑ) and go down the steps, then turn right at the bottom and walk along the metalled lane, passing a few houses on either side. At the end of the lane, continue along the footpath to the river, which you cross by a metal bridge. Follow the enclosed track into woodland and, at the fingerpost, bear right, following the Tweed Walk signs. Your track is wide now and leads you past the front of a little house on the left-hand side.

Maintain your direction down the long straight avenue marked 'Private Road to Barns'. Turn right at the pink tower and walk along the track, before turning left after a few hundred yards at the fingerpost (Point Ⓒ). You get great views of the hills now as you dip down into a small valley. Cross a couple of stiles and walk down to the river, then bear right following the obvious track by the riverside. Your way now takes you over a ladder stile and through a couple of gates until you reach Manor Bridge. Take the steps up on to the bridge then turn right and rejoin Walk 8 at Point ❺.

A Revolutionary Utopia at New Lanark

*A rustic walk through
a model industrial community.*

DISTANCE 6.5 miles (10.4km)   **MINIMUM TIME** 3hrs
ASCENT/GRADIENT 476ft (145m) ▲▲▲   **LEVEL OF DIFFICULTY** ✛✛✛
PATHS Clear riverside tracks and forest paths, a few steep steps
LANDSCAPE Planned industrial town and some stunning waterfalls
SUGGESTED MAP OS Explorer 335 Lanark & Tinto Hills
START/FINISH Grid reference: NS 883426
DOG FRIENDLINESS Mostly off lead
PARKING Main car park above New Lanark
PUBLIC TOILETS Visitor centre, when open

WALK 10 DIRECTIONS

From the car park, walk downhill into the planned industrial village of New Lanark. It was built as a cotton spinning centre in 1785 by David Dale and Richard Arkwright, and is so well preserved that it is now a UNESCO World Heritage Site. It owes its fame to Dale's son-in-law, Robert Owen, who took over its management in 1798 and made it the focus of a revolutionary social experiment. Owen believed in humane capitalism and felt that businesses were more successful if the workers were well treated. Unlike most industrialists of his

day, he did not allow children under ten to work in his mills, and established the world's first nursery school. Owen also disapproved of the cruel treatment of workers and refused to allow corporeal punishment to be used as a form of discipline. His staff were provided with good housing, a co-operative store and free medical care. Owen tried hard to persuade other industrialists to adopt his regime, but failed.

WHILE YOU'RE THERE

The ruins of Corra Castle are home to a colony of Natterer's bats. These medium-sized bats are found throughout Britain. In winter they tend to hibernate in caves and mines, while during the summer they prefer to roost in old stone buildings and barns. Their limbs have a slight pink tinge, giving rise to their nickname – the 'red-armed bat'.

Disillusioned, he sold New Lanark in 1825 and travelled to America to pursue his dream of Utopia on the other side of the Atlantic.

Bear left and walk to the Scottish Wildlife Trust visitor centre. Turn up the stone steps on the left, following the signs to the Falls of Clyde. The path soon goes down some steps to reach the weir, where there's a lookout point.

Continue along the path. You'll pass Bonnington Power Station on your right, where it divides. Take the right-hand path, which takes you into woodland and up some steps. You'll soon come to Corra Linn waterfall, where there is another lookout point. The falls were immortalised in verse by Willian Wordsworth in 1802 and have provided inspiration to many artists including J M W Turner.

WHERE TO EAT AND DRINK

There's a self-service café in the village where you can get baked potatoes, sandwiches, cakes and hot drinks. The Mill Hotel also serves bar snacks.

Your path continues to the right, signposted 'Bonnington Linn, 0.75 miles'. Go up some more steps and follow the track to go under a double line of pylons. Follow the path to reach the weir, cross it, then turn right into the Wildlife Reserve. After 100yds (91m), turn right off the track down a narrow path, which crosses a footbridge and then follows the river, rejoining the main path downstream. Bear right here to reach Corra Castle. Continue walking along by the river, cross a small footbridge, then follow the wide path through the woods. When you meet another path, turn off to the right.

Follow the path to pass houses on your left. At the road turn right, then right again to cross the old bridge, which brings you into a cul de sac. Go through the gate on the right – it looks like someone's drive but it is, in fact, part of the Clyde Walkway.

WHAT TO LOOK OUT FOR

Peregrines nest near the Corra Linn falls from April to June. CCTV now beams live action of the peregrines and Corra Linn waterfall into the Clyde Visitor Centre in New Lanark. Peregrines are a protected species, with only around 800 pairs in Scotland, and are sadly threatened by egg collectors, shooting and poisoning.

Walk past the stables, then turn left through a gate to follow the path along the river. Beyond another gate, continue up some steps beside a water treatment plant and bear right along a tarmac lane. Follow the lane past some houses until you see a sign to Jooker's Johnnie on your left. Just 20yds (18m) further on, turn right down a driveway, then turn right again at a sign indicating the Clyde Walkway.

Your path zig-zags down to the river. At the water's edge turn left, and follow the forest track back to New Lanark. You get some great views of the mills on the way. When the path meets the road turn right, then left at the church for the car park.

Overleaf: Water tumbles down the rock-face at the Falls of Clyde, New Lanark (Walk 10)   35

Remembering the Jacobites at Traquair

You'll find Jacobite connections in an atmospheric old house and a moorland fairy well on this walk.

DISTANCE 7 miles (11.3km)   MINIMUM TIME 3hrs 30min

ASCENT/GRADIENT 1,378ft (420m) ▲▲▲   LEVEL OF DIFFICULTY +++

PATHS Firm, wide moorland tracks, 1 stile

LANDSCAPE Rolling hills and heather-clad moors – some excellent views

SUGGESTED MAP OS Explorer 337 Peebles & Innerleithen

START/FINISH Grid reference: NT 331345

DOG FRIENDLINESS Can run free for long stretches, but on lead near sheep

PARKING Southern Upland Way car park in Traquair, near village hall

PUBLIC TOILETS None on route; nearest in car park at Peebles

There can be few more romantic places in Britain than Traquair House, just a couple of minutes' drive from the start of this walk. It's the oldest continually inhabited house in Scotland and is still owned by the Maxwell Stuart family, who came here in 1491.

Parts of the house date back to the 12th century, although most of the present building was built in 1680. It's a house full of secret stairways and little windows and even has its own brewery, whose origins stretch back to the 16th century. Traquair House is one of those marvellous places that simply ooze atmosphere – largely, I think, because it is still a family home.

All in a Good Cause

The house was always a popular stopping-off point for Scottish monarchs and 27 of them visited over the years, including Mary, Queen of Scots, who stayed here with her husband Darnley in 1566.

The family were traditionally staunch Catholics and when the Protestant William of Orange took the throne in 1689, they joined many others in supporting the Jacobite cause. This demanded that the Stuart King James II (Charles II's brother) be reinstated on the throne and, contrary to popular myth, attracted support among English people as well as Scots. Years of repression and bloodshed followed.

Hiding Out at Traquair

The Jacobite rebellion eventually culminated in the disastrous defeat at Culloden in 1746. You can, of course, visit the site of the battle itself, but it is somehow easier to understand what it must have been like to live during those times when you see the secret priest's room at Traquair. Often called 'priest's holes', these rooms were made in many of the great houses throughout Britain, allowing priests to live in hiding and take Mass for the devout family. The one in Traquair has such a strong atmosphere that it almost feels as if the priest has just stepped out for a moment.

The 4th Earl of Traquair was imprisoned in the Tower of London and sentenced to death for his part in one of the early Jacobite risings. However, he managed to make a story-book escape, when his wife smuggled him out of prison by dressing him as a maid. The cloak he used as his disguise is on display at Traquair. Years later, the 5th Earl was also held prisoner in the Tower for supporting the Jacobites at Culloden.

A Royal Promise

Bonnie Prince Charlie visited Traquair in 1745, passing through the great Bear Gates – so named because of the bear statues that top the gateposts. When the prince left, the 5th Earl wished him a safe journey, closed the gates behind him and promised that they would not be opened again until there was a Stuart monarch on the throne. The gates have remained unopened ever since.

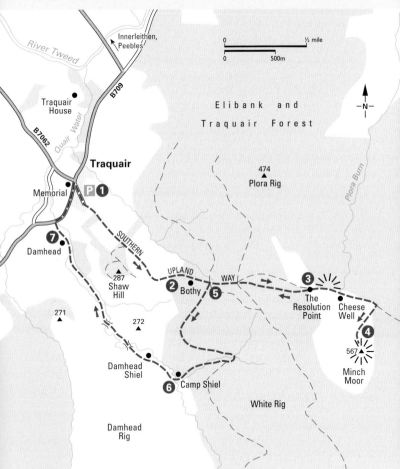

WALK 11 DIRECTIONS

1 From the Southern Upland Way car park, join the tarmac road and walk left away from Traquair village. Continue ahead and then join the gravel track following signs for the Minch Moor. After you go through a gate the track becomes grassier, then you hop over a stile and enter Forestry Commission land.

2 Continue on the obvious track to pass a bothy on the right. When you come to a crossing of tracks, maintain direction, crossing an area of scrub and self-seeded trees. When you reach a forest track, continue ahead, taking a narrow path to the right of a cycleway. The path winds uphill to rejoin the cycle track at The Resolution Point.

WHERE TO EAT AND DRINK

In Innerleithen you can get a drink at the Traquair Arms Hotel. They also do cakes and hot drinks, as well as more substantial meals such as filo parcels, pasta bakes and aubergine cannelloni. There's also a restaurant at Traquair House, as well as a Brewery Shop selling Traquair Jacobite Ale to take home with you.

3 Maintain direction, enjoying great views over Walkerburn to the left. It feels wilder and windier up here, with large tracts of heather-covered moorland by your path. When you reach a marker post, turn right and walk up to the cairn on the Minch Moor – the views should be great on a clear day.

4 From the cairn, retrace your steps back to the main track. before turning left and walking back downhill – stopping to leave some food when you pass the Cheese Well (see What to

WHAT TO LOOK OUT FOR

The cheese well is a freshwater spring marked by two well-weathered stones. It is said that if you pass the well, you should leave a food offering, usually cheese (hence the name), to the fairies who haunt the area. This will ensure you a safe and successful journey.

WHILE YOU'RE THERE

The mineral waters at St Ronan's Well near Innerleithen have been attracting visitors since the 18th century and inspired the eponymous novel by Sir Walter Scott. The well is covered by a pavilion and you can still sample the waters. Guided walks around the well and garden are available to visitors on request.

Look Out For) on the left – it's by the boggy part of the path. Turn left 20yds (18m) beyond The Resolution Point and return downhill across one forest track to reach a second intersection.

5 Turn left now and walk downhill. The landscape soon opens out on the right-hand side giving you pleasant views of the valley and the river winding away. When you reach the apex of a bend, turn right along a grassy path. Follow this as it bears downhill, go through a gate and walk beside Camp Shiel cottage.

6 Go through another gate, cross the burn, then follow the grassy track and pass Damhead Shiel cottage. Go through another gate and follow the path across a bridge over a burn. You'll pass an expanse of scree on the right-hand side, and an ox-bow lake evolving on the left. Cross another bridge and continue to Damhead farm.

7 Walk past the farm and down to the road, then turn right. You'll now cross the burn again and will walk past some cottages on the right-hand side. When you reach the war memorial on the left, turn right and walk up the track to reach the parking place at the start of the walk on the left.

Holy Orders at Jedburgh

*Follow waymarked footpaths
from this historic town.*

DISTANCE 4.5 miles (7.2km)		MINIMUM TIME 3hrs

ASCENT/GRADIENT 295ft (90m) ▲▲▲   LEVEL OF DIFFICULTY ✦✦✦

PATHS *Tracks, meadow paths and some sections of road, 2 stiles*

LANDSCAPE *Gentle hills and fine old abbey*

SUGGESTED MAP *OS Explorer OL16 The Cheviot Hills*

START/FINISH *Grid reference: NT 651204*

DOG FRIENDLINESS *Fair, but keep on lead near sheep and on road*

PARKING *Main car park by tourist information centre*

PUBLIC TOILETS *At car park*

Although it was built back in the 12th century, the beauty and grandeur of Jedburgh Abbey is still clearly evident. It certainly dominates this bustling border town, and sits serene and seemingly untroubled by the hustle and hassle of modern life. It must have seemed still more impressive in medieval times, when the power of the Church was at its height and the population was generally uneducated and superstitious.

The abbey is one of four in the Borders – the others being at Dryburgh, Kelso and Melrose – and all were built after the Norman Conquest. They are stretched across the Borders like a string of ecclesiastical jewels. Jedburgh Abbey is one of the most impressive medieval buildings in Scotland. It was built for French Augustinian canons in 1138 by David I, on the site of an earlier Anglo-Saxon monastery, and was specifically designed to make a visual impact. This was not because the King was exceedingly devout, but was owing to the fact that Jedburgh is very close to the border with England. David needed to make an obvious statement of authority to his powerful Norman neighbours.

Monastic Life

Each of the Border abbeys belonged to a different religious order. The Augustinian canons at Jedburgh were also known as 'Black Canons' owing to the colour of their robes. Unlike monks, canons were all ordained clergymen who were allowed to administer Holy Communion. Dryburgh Abbey was founded by Premonstratensian canons, who wore white robes and lived a more secluded life than the Augustinians. Kelso Abbey, which became one of the largest monasteries in Scotland, belonged to the Benedictine order, while Melrose was founded by Cistercian monks. The Cistercians took their name from the forest of Cîteaux in France, where their first community was established. Often known as 'White Benedictines', Cistercian monks adhered strictly to the Rule of St Benedict. Manual labour in the abbey was carried out by poor, and generally illiterate, lay brothers. These people lived and worshipped separately to the 'choir' monks who devoted their time to reading, writing and private prayer. The Cistercians adhered to a strict regime, designed to purify their lives. They banned the use of practical goods such as bedspreads, combs and even underwear.

Abbeys Under Fire

These medieval abbeys all suffered in the battles that ravaged the Borders for centuries. Jedburgh, for example, was stripped of its roofing lead by Edward I's troops who stayed here during the Wars of Independence. It came under attack many times and was burned by the Earl of Surrey in 1530. After the Reformation, all the abbeys fell into decline and began to decay. Today they remain picturesque reminders of a previous age.

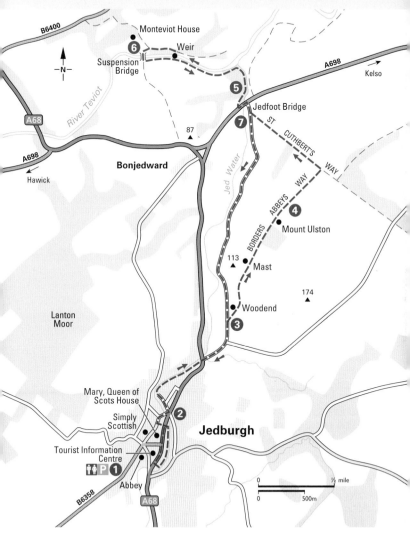

WALK 12 DIRECTIONS

1 From the car park, walk back to the A68. Cross the road into

Duck Row. Take the path on the left to walk beside the river, under an old bridge, then come on to the road. Turn right across the bridge.

WALK 12

2 Turn left, following the sign for Borders Abbeys Way. Where the road divides, turn left and follow the lane beside a builders' yard to join Waterside Walk. When you reach the main road, cross and follow the tarmac lane uphill. Keep straight on, passing a turning on the right, until you reach a fork, just before a farmyard development on the left.

3 Turn right here to walk in front of a small farmhouse called Woodend. Turn left on to a footpath and continue past the front of Mount Ulston house. Your route now runs uphill, taking you past a radio mast. Maintain direction to join the narrow grassy track – this can get very muddy, even in the summer.

4 Continue along this track until you reach the fingerpost at the end, where you turn left to join St Cuthbert's Way. The going becomes much easier now as you

are walking along a wide, firm track. When you reach the tarmac road, turn right and join the main road. Turn left, go over the bridge, then cross the road. You now hop over the crash barrier and go down some steps to continue following St Cuthbert's Way.

5 You're now on a narrow, grassy track, which runs beside the river. You then have to nip over a couple of stiles, before walking across a meadow frequently grazed by sheep. Walk past the weir, then go through the gate to cross the suspension bridge – take care as it can get extremely slippery here.

6 You now pass a sign for Monteviot House and walk through the woods to reach a fingerpost, where you can turn right to enjoy views over the river. If you wish to extend your walk, you can continue along St Cuthbert's Way until it joins the road, then retrace your steps. Whatever you choose, you then retrace your steps back over the suspension bridge, along the riverside and back to the main road. Turn left across a bridge, then immediately right down a tarmac lane.

7 Ignoring the track off to the left, follow the road all the way back to Jedburgh. Cross the A68 and return back along Waterside Walk to the car park.

One of Scotland's Great Scotts at Dryburgh

A gentle walk in the Borders countryside that was much beloved by Sir Walter Scott.

DISTANCE	5 miles (8km) MINIMUM TIME 3hrs
ASCENT/GRADIENT	131ft (40m) ▲▲▲ LEVEL OF DIFFICULTY ✦✦✦
PATHS	Firm woodland and riverside tracks, 3 stiles
LANDSCAPE	Historic abbey and river banks
SUGGESTED MAP	OS Explorer 338 Galashiels, Selkirk & Melrose
START/FINISH	Grid reference: NT 592318
DOG FRIENDLINESS	Keep on lead on Mertoun Estate and by golf course
PARKING	Dryburgh Abbey car park
PUBLIC TOILETS	At car park

Walk anywhere in the Scottish Borders and you are probably following in the footsteps of one of Scotland's most celebrated literary figures – Sir Walter Scott. He travelled widely here, writing marvellous books and poetry that would be described as bestsellers if they were published today. Yet, while everyone has certainly heard of Sir Walter Scott, hardly anyone now reads his books.

Wavering over *Waverley*

The reason for this is almost certainly the somewhat impenetrable nature of the language he uses – impenetrable to non Scots, anyway. Full of enthusiasm, people tend to pick up a copy of *Waverley* (1814), a romantic tale of the Jacobite rebellion, then put it down in defeat after page ten. But those who persist and learn to unravel the old Scots dialect discover tales that were strongly influenced by the ballads, folklore and history of the borderlands – tales that would have died out otherwise.

From Polio to Poetry

Scott was the son of an Edinburgh lawyer but spent a lot of time in the Borders as a child while recuperating from polio. He was fascinated by the stories and ballads he heard and, when he grew older, began to collect material that he later turned into romantic poetry. He was greatly influenced by Robert Burns and became friends with James Hogg, the Ettrick Shepherd (see Walk 2). Scott became a barrister in 1792, but spent his spare time writing poetry. He was appointed Sheriff-Depute of Selkirk in 1799 and in 1811 he moved to Abbotsford, a farmhouse near Melrose, where he lived for the rest of his life. He turned to novel writing, declaring that 'Byron beat me' at poetry.

It was a decision that was to make Scott's fortune – but it was also, ultimately, to cost him his health. After the publication of *Waverley*, he produced several more historical novels, including *Rob Roy* (1817), *The Heart of Midlothian* (1818) and *Ivanhoe* (1819). Scott's novels revived interest in Scottish culture, at a time when it had been in danger of disappearing. In 1818 he discovered the Honours of Scotland, a crown, sword and sceptre, which had been hidden in Edinburgh Castle from the time of Charles II (see Walk 50). And a few years later he was invited to make the arrangements for George IV's visit to Scotland – the King entered wholeheartedly into the spirit of the visit and delighted the crowds by wearing a kilt teamed with some natty pink tights.

Scott should have been able to live in relative wealth and comfort, but in 1825 his publishing house collapsed and he was left with enormous debts. His wife died the same year. Scott worked furiously to pay off his debts, but his health suffered and in 1832 he died at Abbotsford. He is buried in the ruins of Dryburgh Abbey.

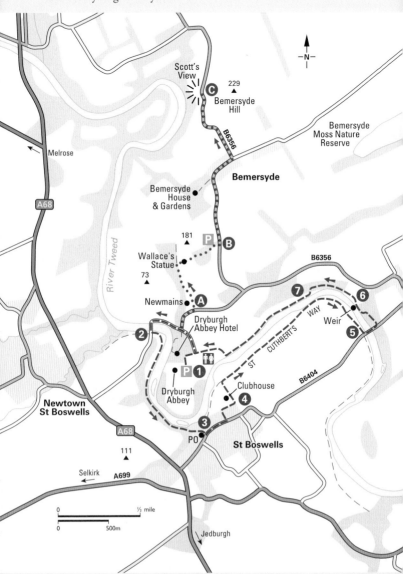

WALK 13 DIRECTIONS

❶ From the car park at the abbey, walk back to join the road. Pass the entrance to the Dryburgh Abbey Hotel and then walk down the dead-end lane in front of you. You'll soon see the river and, at the end of the road, continue along a footpath and bypass, before crossing the bridge over the River Tweed.

❷ Turn left immediately and join St Cuthbert's Way. This waymarked trail now leads along the river banks. At some points there are steps, tiny footbridges and patches of boardwalk to assist you. Continue to follow this trail which eventually takes you past two small islands in the river, where it then leads away from the river bank.

WHILE YOU'RE THERE

Abbotsford, west of Melrose, was Sir Walter Scott's home from 1811 until his death. He spent an enormous amount of money turning the original farmhouse into the home you see today. Scott's influence can be felt everywhere, from the library, which contains over 9,000 rare books, to the historic relics, such as Rob Roy's gun. You can visit both the house and grounds and there's a handy tea room too.

❸ Follow the trail on to a tarmac track, then left. At the main road in St Boswells go left again and continue to follow the trail signs, passing a post office and later Scott's View chippy on your left. After house No. 101, turn left down Bravheads Road and then go to your right along a tarmac track at the end.

❹ Follow this, then turn left and walk past the golf clubhouse.

Continue walking for a few paces, then turn right and follow St Cuthbert's Way as it hugs the golf course. You now continue by the golf course until your track eventually brings you back down to the river bank. Walk past the weir and up to the bridge.

WHERE TO EAT AND DRINK

The Dryburgh Abbey Hotel has a bar and restaurant that is open to non-residents. However if you want more choice, drive into Melrose where there are several pubs and restaurants offering everything from French food to traditional Scottish dishes. Perhaps the best known is Burts Hotel, an 18th-century inn which serves good bar meals and offers a choice of 50 single malts.

❺ Go up the steps and cross the bridge (take care, there is no footway), then turn sharp left and walk towards the cottages. Before the cottages, go left, over the footbridge, then turn right along the river bank to walk in front of them. At the weir, take the steps that run up to the right, nip over the stile and into a field.

❻ Go left now and keep to the track through woodland down to the river bank, following the waymarked trail.

❼ Follow the river, keeping an eye out for fish leaping up to feed from the water's surface. You'll cross a stile, then pass a greenhouse on your left. Climb another stile here, turn right, walk past the toilets and, at the house ahead, turn left and walk back into the car park.

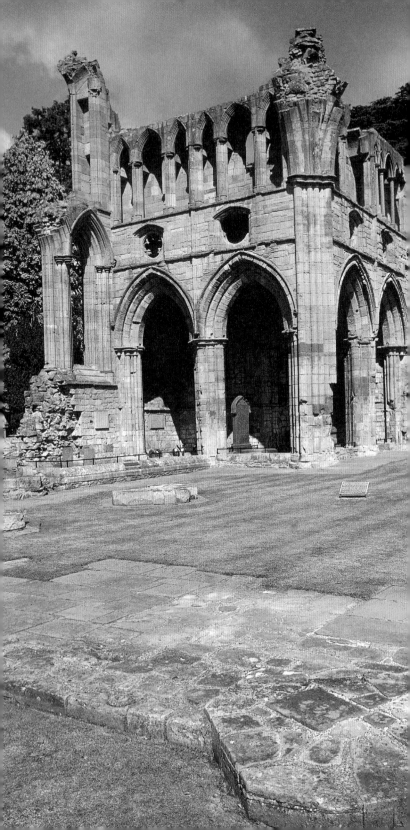

A Diversion to Scott's View

A linear walk to see the Eildon Hills from Sir Walter Scott's favourite spot.

See map and information panel for Walk 13

> **DISTANCE** *3.5 miles (5.7km)* **MINIMUM TIME** *1hr*
> **ASCENT/GRADIENT** *394ft (120m)* ▲▲▲ **LEVEL OF DIFFICULTY** ✦✦✦

WALK 14 DIRECTIONS (Walk 13 option)

You can do this extension at either the beginning or the end of the walk. From the parking place in Dryburgh (Point ❶ on the main walk) walk back to join the road, pass the entrance to the Dryburgh Abbey Hotel and follow the main road as it bends to the right. Just past the house called Newmains (Point Ⓐ), turn left and follow the public footpath uphill. When you come to an intersection, turn sharp right and follow the path up to the statue of William Wallace.

The statue is enormous and made of red sandstone. It's inscribed with the words 'Great Patriot Hero'. It's worth bringing your camera with you, as the views from this spot on a clear day are great. Walk in front of the statue and continue to follow the path as it runs downhill. It is a clear, wide track from now and brings you down to a small car park (Point Ⓑ). Turn left now and walk along the road.

Eventually you'll pass the entrance to Bemersyde House and Gardens, once the home of Earl Haig. Continue on the main road as it bears right and then left until you finally reach the wide lay-by that marks Scott's View (Point Ⓒ). There's a geographical indicator here pointing out places of interest. The view is amazing and you can see the Eildon Hills that so inspired Sir Walter Scott. Scott played a large part in encouraging a love of wild landscapes by immortalising them in his works.

To return, retrace your steps back to the car park, to rejoin the main walk at Point ❶.

WHILE YOU'RE THERE

Dryburgh Abbey, set on the banks of the Tweed, is the most romantic of all the Border abbeys and simply begs to have its picture taken. It is hardly surprising that it was chosen as the burial place for Sir Walter Scott. However, few people are aware that a rather less celebrated Scot is buried here – Field Marshal Earl Haig. Haig was the commander of the British Army in the First World War, when millions died under his command on the battlefields of northern France. Following the Armistice, Bemersyde was donated to him by a nation grateful for his service, but Haig himself never came to terms with the cost of victory in terms of human lives. He devoted the rest of his life to charities for ex-servicemen and their families, founding the British Legion in 1921.

A March Around the Marches of Lauder

An exhilarating walk in open country surrounding the historic town of Lauder, where an ancient tradition is observed each year.

> **DISTANCE** 4 miles (6.4km) **MINIMUM TIME** 2hrs
> **ASCENT/GRADIENT** 525ft (160m) ▲▲▲ **LEVEL OF DIFFICULTY** ✦✦✦
> **PATHS** Grassy tracks, open fields
> **LANDSCAPE** Rolling hills and farmland
> **SUGGESTED MAP** OS Explorer 338 Galashiels, Selkirk & Melrose
> **START/FINISH** Grid reference: NT 531475
> **DOG FRIENDLINESS** Keep on lead near livestock
> **PARKING** High Street in Lauder
> **PUBLIC TOILETS** By Market Place in Lauder

WALK 15 DIRECTIONS

Like all towns in the Borders, Lauder is steeped in tradition. The town dates back to the 14th century and is a fine example of a medieval Scottish 'burgh'. The Tolbooth in the Market Place, for instance, was built so that tolls could be collected from people selling goods at the market. However, it is more noted for its associations with witchcraft, as the ground floor was used as a jail until 1843 and in earlier times witches were said to have been burned at the stake here.

Place names such as Dunking Pool near the town are reminders that witches were often tried by being tied up and dunked into deep water. If they drowned they were considered innocent – if they survived they were guilty and burned at the stake.

From the Market Place, walk east to turn down Mill Wynd (it's by the church). Walk past the housing estate, then bear right at the fingerpost by the car park and take the path to the left of the ruined barn to join the Southern Upland Way. This waymarked walk was Britain's first coast-to-coast footpath and runs for 212 miles (341km) from Portpatrick in the south-west to Cockburnspath in the east. It's quite a challenging walk, with some long and demanding stretches.

The wide, grassy track now leads gently uphill, past a mobile phone mast and up to a gate. Go through the gate and continue ahead. The path is clear and firm underfoot and you're now walking with a golf course on your left and re-establishing the town's boundaries and protecting common land. Today the event involves hundreds of riders galloping wildly across the countryside following the 'Cornet' who carries the town's standard. It takes place early in August.

a deep river gully on your right – which looks really splendid as the sun begins to set.

You soon pass a small copse on the left-hand side. Continue walking past the copse and maintain direction until you descend towards a ladder stile. Don't cross this stile but bear to the right, leaving the Southern Upland Way.

A narrow path here goes downhill, bearing right to a footbridge across the burn. Once across the bridge, you join a clear route that runs uphill through the bracken.

This is lovely open countryside and it's easy to imagine people galloping past on horses. Lauder, like all the Border towns, has a Common Riding every year. Also known as the Riding of the Marches (boundaries), this is an ancient ritual dating back to the Middle Ages when men would ride out to 'beat the bounds',

Approaching the crest of the hill, you bear right and join another track that leads to a small copse. Walk past the copse, and then continue across the field until you reach a stone wall. Turn right here, following the waymarked path with the wall to your left. As you start to descend, you have a fine view ahead of you of the town of Lauder with the turrets of Thirlestane Castle beyond. Go through a kissing gate and turn right, following the waymarked route down into the valley with a wall on your right. You now go through a metal gate and over a footbridge across the burn. On the far bank, you fork right up some wooden steps, then turn left along a clear path, which descends slowly back down to the level of the burn. Continue through a gate, with the burn to your left and across a footbridge. Turn right here along a good firm track past some houses on the left and continue through a gate on to the road. Turn left here to return to the town centre.

The Gypsy Palace of Kirk Yetholm

*This energetic walk takes you
over the border to England.*

DISTANCE 7 miles (11.3km)   **MINIMUM TIME** 4hrs 30min

ASCENT/GRADIENT 1,600ft (488m) ▲▲▲   **LEVEL OF DIFFICULTY** +++

PATHS Wide tracks and waymarked paths, one short overgrown section, 3 stiles

LANDSCAPE Rolling open hills with panoramic views

SUGGESTED MAP OS Explorer OL16 The Cheviot Hills

START/FINISH Grid reference: NT 839276

DOG FRIENDLINESS Excellent, though keep on lead near sheep

PARKING Car park outside Kirk Yetholm at junction of Pennine Way
and St Cuthbert's Way

PUBLIC TOILETS None en route

This is such a lovely walk that you'll want to do it again and again. It's easy to follow, the paths are good and the views have a definite 'wow' factor – so do try to save it for a clear day so that you get the full effect. The walk includes the added thrill of crossing the border from Scotland into England – no, you won't need your passport.

The little village of Kirk Yetholm was noted as a gypsy settlement from at least 1695, although they were probably there before that, as they were in Scotland by the early 16th century. Gypsies were generally regarded with suspicion as they had a reputation for stealing and aggression – it was even said that they kidnapped children and brought them up as their own. However, they were also said to be loyal to those who helped them and never broke their word.

A Royal Family Home

No one is quite sure how the gypsies came to settle in Kirk Yetholm, although many moved to the wild areas of the Borders where they could hide in the hills, after a law was passed in Scotland in 1609 making it legal to kill them. Some say that a young gypsy boy saved the life of a local laird, who showed his thanks by building several homes for gypsies in the village; others, that a gypsy boy helped a local laird to recover a horse that had been stolen and was rewarded with a house in Kirk Yetholm. There were several homes for gypsies in the village, with one cottage being specially built for the royal family – it's called the Gypsy Palace today.

The gypsy royal family had the surname Faa. The first king in Kirk Yetholm was Patrick Faa, who married Jean Gordon. Jean was a powerful character who lived a wild life. Three of her sons were hanged for sheep stealing and she was banned from Kirk Yetholm after attacking another woman. She was said to be the inspiration for Sir Walter Scott's character, Meg Merrilees. She was later immortalised by Keats in his eponymous poem that began: 'Old Meg she was a gypsy; and lived upon the moors: her bed it was the brown heath turf, and her house was out of doors'.

KIRK YETHOLM

The last queen of the gypsies was Esther Faa-Blythe who once said the scattered village was 'sae mingle-mangle that ane micht think it was either built on a dark nicht, or sawn on a windy ane'. Her son, Charles Blythe, was crowned king in 1898 – but the gypsy way of life had gone by then. Today only the Palace remains.

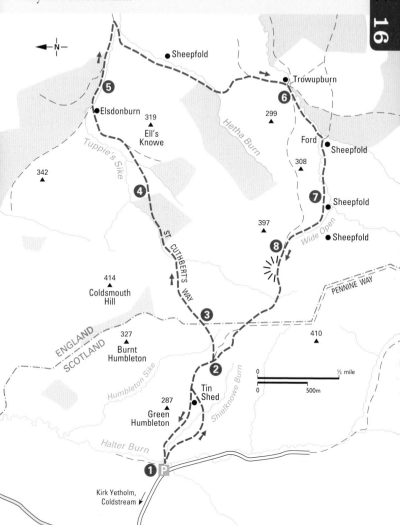

WALK 16 DIRECTIONS

❶ From the car park cross the burn by the footbridge, following the signs to St Cuthbert's Way. Bear right to follow the obvious track uphill, keeping the Shielknowe Burn below on your left. Eventually the track crosses the burn, then continues uphill, skirting the edge of Green Humbleton hill and eventually reaching a fingerpost.

❷ This is the place where St Cuthbert's Way splits from the Pennine Way. Take the grassy path on the left to follow St Cuthbert's

51

Way. Continue following this path as it winds uphill, then takes you to a fingerpost by a wall, which marks the border between Scotland and England.

❸ Follow the path slantwise over the ridgeline ahead, then straight down into the valley beyond. At the valley floor, cross the right-hand stream to the near corner of a plantation. Cross a stile into the forest, where the path keeps near the foot of the trees, then joins the fence alongside the stream, before slanting slightly right into more open forest of pine. You'll soon walk down an avenue of trees and leave the wood by another stile.

❹ Keep ahead across the field. From the gate at its far side a track starts that crosses a small stream, heads briefly uphill, then winds downs to reach Elsdonburn farm. Turn left between the farm buildings and follow the track as it bends round to the right. It becomes a tarred lane, with a conifer wood on its left and the burn on its right.

❺ Follow this tarred track across a cattle grid to a signpost. Here you leave St Cuthbert's Way to take the tarred track on the right signed 'Trowupburn'. Follow this, passing a sheepfold and then a conifer plantation. The track eventually winds upwards, skirts a hill, then descends to Trowupburn farmhouse. Continue to walk past the farm buildings then bear right to a fingerpost.

❻ Go through the gate here and follow the sign 'Border Ridge 1.5'. Wander along this wide grassy track then cross the ford next to the very large sheepfold. Head upstream with the burn now on your right, then cross the burn again, nip over the stile and join the sheep track that bears left through the bracken.

❼ Walk round the hill and, when you are directly above a sheepfold on the left, bear right so that the Wide Open burn is on your left, the sheepfold behind you. Work your way uphill through the bracken to the head of the burn until you reach a fence on the higher ground.

❽ Go through the gate at the corner and take the green path ahead across open ground. Walk around the head of a stream valley (the stream drops to the right) to the wall and fence marking the border with Scotland. Cross a stile and bear right to a Pennine Way fingerpost. Here, bear left and follow the green path and waymarkers downhill and past the fingerpost of St Cuthbert's Way (Point ❷). Keep ahead above a tin shed, on a path leading down to the footbridge at the start.

The Cleverness of Duns

Quiet lanes take you through gentle countryside past ancient monuments to the romantic battlements of Duns Castle.

DISTANCE 4.5 miles (7.2km)   **MINIMUM TIME** 2hrs

ASCENT/GRADIENT 250ft (76m) ▲▲▲   **LEVEL OF DIFFICULTY** ✦✦✦

PATHS Mostly firm tracks and woodland paths

LANDSCAPE Parkland, lake and mixed woodland

SUGGESTED MAP OS Explorer 346 Berwick-upon-Tweed

START/FINISH Grid reference: NT 787538

DOG FRIENDLINESS Keep dogs on lead; be considerate of ground-nesting birds

PARKING Long-stay car park off Market Square, Duns

PUBLIC TOILETS In South Street, Duns

Truth, as Oscar Wilde observed, is never pure and rarely simple. The same might be said about some landscapes, as this intriguing walk makes plain. Along the way, you will come across a fascinating record of the past from prehistoric earthworks to a castle that is still a lived-in home. But almost nothing that you see is quite what it appears. Enigmas and legends enshroud the ancient sites; the castle has been altered to enhance its romance, and monuments perpetuate some very doubtful tales. Even the quite natural-looking lake you pass was in fact artfully designed.

Unreliable History

At the start of the walk, a short climb takes you to the hilltop of Duns Law. It's worth it for the views alone, which on a clear day extend down to the Cheviots and Lindsifarne. An Iron Age settlement existed here more than 2,000 years ago, although nothing but faint banks and ditches now remain. A smaller, rectangular enclosure is of much more recent date, forming the stockade in which General Leslie mustered his army of Covenanters in 1639 when Charles I attempted to impose the English Prayer Book on Scotland. You can even see the very stone on which, according to tradition, the Covenanters raised their standard. Two other monuments that you will see along the route are equally the products of tales passed down by word of mouth rather than of documented history. Just off the path back down the hill (a sign points you in the right direction) a cairn claims to mark the spot where the town of Duns originally stood until destroyed by an English raid. But in fact the town has always been exactly where it is today, so perhaps the story may derive from old folk tales about the prehistoric settlement. Then, near the castle gatehouse, another cairn claims to mark the precise birthplace of the medieval philosopher Duns Scotus. In truth, almost nothing of his early life is known.

Landscape Design

Although Duns Castle is not open to the public, its romantic, battlemented towers can be glimpsed from many points along the route. The keep was

DUNS

originally built in 1320, during the reign of Robert the Bruce, but much of what you see today was designed by the architect James Gillespie Graham in the 1820s. The park, including the delightful lake that rejoices in the name of Hen Poo, was also laid out in its present form during the early 19th century, although the avenue of limes that you pass on the last stage of the walk was planted in the 1690s. The trees were blown down in a gale in 1880 and even then they were considered of such venerable significance that they were hauled back upright and saved.

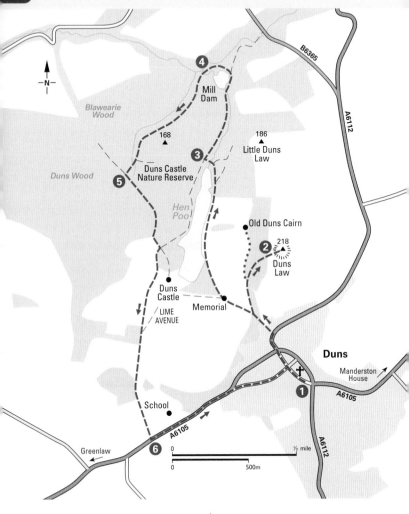

WALK 17 DIRECTIONS

❶ From the car park, return to Market Square and continue straight ahead up Castle Street. Cross the main road to follow the continuation of Castle Street, bearing left to enter Duns Castle

Estate through an arched gateway. Walk down the drive and after 50yds (46m) turn right up a flight of wooden steps. Follow the path uphill and through a gate to reach the summit of Duns Law, with its excellent views of East Berwickshire on a clear day.

④ Turn left to cross the bridge and climb a flight of rough timber steps. When you reach a wooden bench, bear right to follow the waymarked 'Colonel's Walk'. When you reach an intersection, after approximately 0.5 mile (800m), turn right (signposted to Duns) and continue 100yds (91m) to another intersection.

② From the hilltop, follow your route back down the hill (a sign half-way down points to the alleged site of Old Duns). On reaching the drive, turn right, then fork right at the memorial to Duns Scotus. Follow the drive along the shore of Hen Poo, then fork left through a gate on to a rougher track to the head of the lake, where the path swings left to reach a T-junction.

③ Turn right here to follow the track along a wooded valley and past a pond, Mill Dam, which formerly provided power for the estate sawmill. Shortly beyond the pond, turn left up a woodland path and continue for 100yds (91m) to a footbridge crossing a small stream.

⑤ Turn left here (again signed to Duns) and follow the driveway until you reach a crossroads. Turn right here, following the waymarked route. After passing Duns Castle and the lime avenue, continue down the estate road until you eventually come to the main road.

⑥ Turn left here and follow the pavement back to Duns. As the main road bears left, continue straight ahead along South Street to reach Market Square, where you turn right to return to the car park at the start of the walk.

A Windy Walk to St Abb's Head

*A refreshing walk along the cliffs
to see some local wildife.*

DISTANCE *4 miles (6.4km)*	**MINIMUM TIME** *1hr 30min*
ASCENT/GRADIENT *443ft (135m)* ▲▲▲	**LEVEL OF DIFFICULTY** ✦✦✦

PATHS *Clear footpaths and established tracks*

LANDSCAPE *Dramatic cliff tops and lonely lighthouse*

SUGGESTED MAP *OS Explorer 346 Berwick-upon-Tweed*

START/FINISH *Grid reference: NT 913674*

DOG FRIENDLINESS *They'll love the fresh air, but keep on lead by cliffs*

PARKING *At visitor centre*

PUBLIC TOILETS *At visitor centre*

St Abb's Head is one of those places that people forget to visit. You only ever seem to hear it mentioned on the shipping forecast – and its name is generally followed by a rather chilly outlook – along the lines of 'north-easterly five, continuous light drizzle, poor'. In fact you could be forgiven for wondering if it even exists or is simply a mysterious expanse of sea – like Dogger, Fisher or German Bight.

But St Abb's Head does exist, as you'll find out on this lovely windswept walk which will rumple your hair and leave the salty tang of the sea lingering on your lips. The dramatic cliffs, along which you walk to reach the lonely lighthouse, form an ideal home for thousands of nesting seabirds as they provide superb protection from mammalian predators. Birds you might spot on this walk include guillemots, razorbills, kittiwakes, herring gulls, shags and fulmars – as well as a few puffins. Guillemots and razorbills are difficult to differentiate, as they're both black and white, and have an upright stance – rather like small, perky penguins. However, you should be able to spot the difference if you've got binoculars as razorbills have distinctive blunt beaks. Both birds belong to the auk family, the most famous member of which is probably the great auk, which went the way of the dodo and became extinct in 1844 – a victim of the contemporary passion for egg collecting.

Luckily no egg collector could scale these cliffs, which are precipitous and surrounded by treacherous seas. Do this walk in the nesting season (May to July) and you may well see young birds jumping off the high cliff ledge into the open sea below. Even though they can't yet fly, as their wings are little more than stubs, the baby birds are nevertheless excellent swimmers and have a better chance of survival in the water than in their nests – where they could fall prey to marauding gulls. Neither razorbills nor guillemots are particularly agile in the air, but they swim with the ease of seals, using their wings and feet to propel and steer their sleek little bodies as they fish beneath the waves.

While the steep cliffs are home to most of the seabirds round St Abb's Head, the low, flat rocks below are also used by wildlife, as they are the favoured nesting site of shags. These large black birds are almost indistinguishable from cormorants – except for the distinctive crest on their heads that gives them a quizzical appearance. They tend to fly low over the water, in contrast to the graceful fulmars that frequently soar along the cliff tops as you walk, hitching a ride on convenient currents of air.

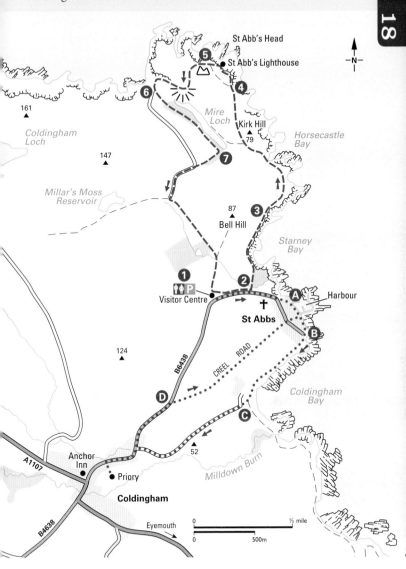

WALK 18 DIRECTIONS

❶ From the car park, take the path that runs past the information board and the play area. Walk past the visitor centre, then take the footpath on the left, parallel to the main road. At the end of the path turn left and go through a gate – you'll immediately get great views of the sea.

❷ Follow the track, pass the sign to Starney Bay and continue, passing fields on your left-hand side. Your track now winds around the edge of the bay – to your right is the little harbour at St Abbs. The track then winds around the cliff edge, past dramatic rock formations and eventually to some steps.

❸ Walk down the steps, then follow the grassy track as it bears left, with a fence on the left. Go up a slope, through a gate and maintain direction on the obvious grassy track. The path soon veers away from the cliff edge, past high ground on the right, then runs up a short, steep slope to a crossing of tracks, passing a butterfly haven on the right.

❹ Maintain direction by keeping to the coastal path which runs up

a slope. You'll soon get great views of the St Abb's lighthouse ahead, dramatically situated on the cliff's edge. Continue to the lighthouse and walk in front of the lighthouse buildings and down to join a tarmac road. Take care as this path is steep and eroded.

❺ Follow the road down to the bottom of the hill, then 50yds (46m) before a cattle grid, turn left down a narrow path.

❻ Continue along the path and cross over a stile. The path now runs through scrub and woodland along the edge of a loch. Continue along the path to an intersection with a track.

❼ Turn right along the wide track and walk up to the road. Go left now and continue to cross a cattle grid. When you reach a bend in the road, follow the tarmac track as it bears left. You'll soon go through a gate, then pass some cottages before reaching the car park on the left-hand side.

And on to the Village of Coldingham

A loop to St Abbs harbour and peaceful Coldingham.

See map and information panel for Walk 18

DISTANCE 2.5 miles (4km) **MINIMUM TIME** 1hr

ASCENT/GRADIENT 197ft (60m) ▲▲▲ **LEVEL OF DIFFICULTY** ✚✚✚

WALK 19 DIRECTIONS
(Walk 18 option)

From Point ❶ of the main walk, walk past the car park and along the road, following the safe footpaths on either side of the road, to pass the church. Continue down to reach the pretty little harbour (Point 🅐) in the village of St Abbs, then climb the steps to the right of Ebbcarr's Café and turn left along Seaview Terrace to reach a large white house on the headland. Here (Point 🅑) follow the coastal footpath, signposted 'to Coldingham Sands'. It's a solid track, dotted with seats so you can sit and enjoy the view. When you reach the beach of Coldingham Bay, bear right on to the track that swings uphill.

You will come out at a post-box at St Vedas Hotel. Take the footpath (Point 🅒) that runs parallel to the road and follow it into Coldingham. Turn left here if you want to visit the priory in the village. If not, turn right towards St Abbs. At a lay-by where the road bends to the left, turn right to join the Creel Road (Point 🅓) and follow it all the way back to St Abbs.

This path, lined with ancient banks and hedges, was used for well over a thousand years by local fishermen and the monks of Coldingham Priory. At the end of the path, turn left and retrace your steps to the car park at the start of the main walk.

WHILE YOU'RE THERE

Coldingham and St Abbs seem like sleepy little places, yet for centuries they were busy settlements and important religious centres. A Bronze Age cemetery was discovered near Coldingham village and Roman pottery and glass beads have also been found. In AD 635, an early Christian missionary – possibly St Finnian – came here from Iona. He founded an ecclesiastical centre, either at St Abb's Head or in Coldingham, and was followed by St Ebba, sister of King Oswy of Northumbria (from whom St Abbs takes its name). Some think that she had turned to religious life in order to escape an arranged marriage – whatever the reason for her arrival, she soon established a monastery at Kirk Hill on St Abb's Head. Vikings destroyed this in the 9th century – all that remains today are faint outlines of buildings in the turf. Nearby Coldingham Priory was founded in 1098 by King Edgar of Scotland. It was frequently damaged in border conflicts with England and almost destroyed by Cromwell in 1648. The priory was rebuilt after the Restoration and still functions as a church today.

Dunbar – John Muir's Home Town

WALK 20

This easy walk takes you to a coastal country park, passing the childhood home of the conservationist John Muir.

DISTANCE *5 miles (8km)* **MINIMUM TIME** *1hr 45min*

ASCENT/GRADIENT *49ft (15m)* ▲▲▲ **LEVEL OF DIFFICULTY** +++

PATHS *Town streets and wide firm tracks, some soft sand*

LANDSCAPE *Golden sands and rugged rocks*

SUGGESTED MAP *OS Explorer 351 Dunbar & North Berwick*

START/FINISH *Grid reference: NT 680788*

DOG FRIENDLINESS *On lead by golf course and in town, can run free on beach*

PARKING *Car park in Station Road*

PUBLIC TOILETS *By leisure centre in Dunbar*

WALK 20 DIRECTIONS

This walk takes you through the little town of Dunbar and along the coast to John Muir Country Park, a large area that encompasses many different habitats. Dunbar was a traditional Scottish seaside resort and still retains a bucket-and-spade appeal, making it popular with families.

Turn right out of Station Road, then left down the High Street. You'll soon pass an attractive statue of a young John Muir, which stands outside the town museum. John Muir was born in the town in 1838 and lived here for 11 years, until his family emigrated to America, settling in Wisconsin. Muir had always loved wildlife and after he nearly lost his sight in an industrial accident (up to then he had been an ingenious inventor), he resolved to dedicate his life to protecting nature. He travelled widely and explored much of the American west, particularly around Yosemite. He became a farmer and was a pioneering conservationist,

WHAT TO LOOK FOR

Dunbar Town House Museum is one of the oldest buildings in the town. Dating from the 16th century, it once served as the town's council chamber, court house and prison. Displays cover many aspects of Dunbar's rich history and the exterior is at present being restored to its original medieval appearance.

campaigning vigorously for a national park in America. His ideas were eventually approved and Yosemite National Park was created. Muir continued to promote the idea of conservation and wrote a number of books including *Our National Parks* (1901) and *The Yosemite* (1912).

Further down the street you pass John Muir House, on the left-hand side of the road. This was Muir's childhood home. A bit further down the street is the tourist information centre. When you reach the bottom of the street bear left and walk past the leisure centre, then turn right down a flight of steps and bear left around

WHERE TO EAT AND DRINK

In Dunbar itself there are several pubs and a choice of Italian restaurants, whilst Graze in the High Street offers coffees and snacks. If you really want a treat, drive further along the coast to Greywalls, a swish hotel in a 1920s country house with a garden designed by Gertrude Jekyll. They serve good tea and shortbread.

the bay. Ignore the first steps up to your left, then turn sharp left up a second flight of steps that lead under a small arch. John Muir had fond memories of the coastline here – and particularly of some very dramatic storms. He once wrote: 'I loved to wander… along the sea-shore to gaze at the shells and seaweeds… and best of all to watch the waves in awful storms thundering on the black headlands and craggy ruins of the old Dunbar Castle…' (*The Story of My Boyhood and Youth*, 1913).

You're now on a wide firm track, with the sea to your right. As you walk you'll pass a war memorial and then some striking rock formations. Your path soon brings you up to a viewpoint with a spectacular panorama across the Firth, taking in Berwick Law, the Bass Rock and the Isle of Mey.

Continue now to go down a flight of steps on the left-hand side, which takes you on to a golf course. Walk round the edge of the course, past the clubhouse on the left-hand side and round the shore. When you reach the holiday chalets there's a lovely sandy beach on your right-hand side, with a bridge on to the sands.

Continue along the lane, past a car-park and a rose garden, then turn right to follow a broad track

that runs past ponds and reed beds. At the end turn left, then go over the wooden footbridge on the right. Once you're over the bridge, turn right and then left, following the track that hugs the wall. The sands of Belhaven Bay are now on your right. Your way now takes you into the woods or you can follow the shoreline along the dunes – as you prefer. In the summer you might spot skylarks or lapwings in the dunes. During the winter keep an eye out for birds such as wigeon, bar-tailed godwit and whooper swan.

WHILE YOU'RE THERE

The Scottish Seabird Centre in North Berwick is a great place to take children. It's a bit like a hi-tech bird hide, as there are screens displaying live pictures of the gannet colony that lives on the Bass Rock out in the Firth of Forth. You can control the cameras yourself from the centre, zooming in and panning as you choose. In spring you can also watch puffins and in winter the cameras are focused on a nearby seal colony.

Walk to the end of the wood, then retrace your steps to cross the small footbridge again. Turn left, walk back along the track by the pool and then turn left. After a few paces, turn right to walk along Back Road, a long straight residential street. At the end of the street turn right, walk past the leisure centre again and back along the High Street to your starting place.

Soldiers and Saints on the Pentlands

A lovely, bracing walk across the hills and past Edinburgh's reservoirs.

DISTANCE 7 miles (11.3km)	**MINIMUM TIME** 3hrs
ASCENT/GRADIENT 837ft (255m) ▲▲▲	**LEVEL OF DIFFICULTY** ✦✦✦

PATHS Wide firm tracks, short stretches can be muddy, 3 stiles
LANDSCAPE Reservoirs, fields and hills
SUGGESTED MAP OS Explorer 344 Pentland Hills
START/FINISH Grid reference: NT 212679
DOG FRIENDLINESS Good, but beware of ground-nesting birds
PARKING Car park at end of Bonaly Road, beyond Bonaly Tower
PUBLIC TOILETS None on route

Although this walk starts just beyond Edinburgh's busy city bypass, you'll soon think that you're miles from the city. The Pentlands are an uncompromising range of hills, which clasp the city in their craggy, green arms. Their peaks rise 1,500ft (457m) above the sea and offer many great walks where you can easily escape the crowds.

This walk takes you past several reservoirs, which keep Scotland's capital supplied with water. The first you pass is Torduff Reservoir, which was built in 1851 and is 72ft (22m) deep. Later on you come down to Glencorse Reservoir. Beneath its waters are concealed the remains of the Chapel of St Katherine's (or Catherine's) in the Hopes. This dates back to the 13th century and the reign of Robert the Bruce. In the unlikely event that it's been extremely dry and the waters are shallow, you might even see it peering out above the surface.

By coincidence (or perhaps not), in Mortonhall, on the other side of the bypass, is the site of St Catherine's Balm Well, or Oily Well. Tradition has it that St Catherine travelled through here carrying holy oil from Mount Sinai. She dropped a little and the well appeared in answer to her prayers. The oily water was said to heal skin diseases and attracted many pilgrims. The nearby suburb of Liberton is a corruption of 'leper town'. A modern explanation for the oily water was deposits of paraffin shale. James VI visited the spot in 1617 and ordered that the well be protected by a building. This was destroyed by Cromwell's troops when they camped on the surrounding hills in 1650. Cromwell, who had been helped to victory in England by the Scottish Covenanters, had fallen out with them after they decided to recognise Charles II as King.

The Pentlands are full of similar memories. The Camus Stone near Farmilehead commemorates a battle fought against the Danes. And in 1666, General Dalyell of The Binns (an ancestor of MP Tam Dalyell) beat a Covenanting force at Rullion Green on these hills, crushing the so-called Pentland rising. These days you may still see soldiers on the Pentlands, for there are army firing ranges at Castlelaw, while recruits from barracks at Glencorse and Redford are often put through their paces on the hills.

Lord Cockburn's Inspiration

At the start of the walk you'll pass Bonaly Tower, once the home of Lord Cockburn (1779–1854), writer and judge, who was inspired by his glorious surroundings to pen the words: 'Pentlands high hills raise their heather-crowned crest, Peerless Edina expands her white breast, Beauty and grandeur are blent in the scene, Bonnie Bonally lies smiling between.'

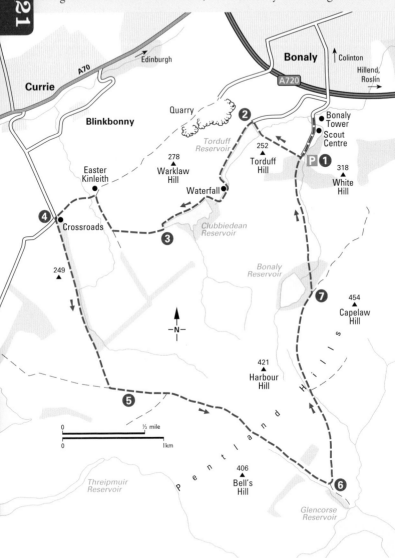

WALK 21 DIRECTIONS

1 From the car park, go through the gate and take the right-hand path, signposted 'Tordruff Reservoir'. Beyond a wooden gate, the path crosses over the reservoir dam to intersect with a tarmac lane.

2 Turn left along the lane, keeping Torduff Reservoir on your

PENTLAND HILLS

left-hand side. When you reach the top of the reservoir, walk over the little bridge and follow the metalled track as it bends round to the right beside a waterfall. Walk under a line of electricity pylons, and go over a small bridge, passing a water chute on your left-hand side, and continue past Clubbiedean Reservoir.

3 Your path now bears right, with fields on either side. Pass under another line of pylons and walk to Easter Kinleith farm. Now follow the lane as it bends back to the left, signposted 'Harlaw'. Pass a sign for Poets' Glen and continue ahead, over a bridge and on to a large white house on the left-hand side called Crossroads.

4 Turn left. Follow the track past a conifer plantation on your left-hand side, then go through a small gate. Continue walking ahead until you reach an intersection. Turn left through a gate, which is signposted to Glencorse.

5 Follow the path across the moor and up into the hills, where you cross a stone stile. Continue in the same direction until you come to a copse of conifers on the right-hand side, with Glencorse Reservoir ahead. Turn left at this point, following the sign to Colinton by Bonaly.

6 Walk uphill and maintain direction to go through a metal gate. The track now narrows and takes you through the hills, until it eventually opens out. Continue in the same direction to reach a fence encircling conifers. Keep the fence on your left and walk down to a gate on the left-hand side.

7 Turn left through the gate. Walk past Bonaly Reservoir, then through a kissing gate and walk downhill, getting good views over Edinburgh as you descend. When you reach a wooden gate, go through and continue ahead, walking downhill, with trees on either side. Go through another kissing gate and follow the tarmac path ahead to return to the car park and the start of the walk.

The Romance of Rosslyn Glen

Tree-lined paths take you beside a river to a very special ancient chapel in this glorious glen.

DISTANCE *5 miles (8km)*   MINIMUM TIME *2hrs 30min*

ASCENT/GRADIENT *279ft (85m)* ▲▲▲   LEVEL OF DIFFICULTY ✦✦✦

PATHS *Generally good, but can be muddy and slippery*

LANDSCAPE *Woodland and fields, short sections of road*

SUGGESTED MAP *OS Explorer 344 Pentland Hills*

START/FINISH *Grid reference: NT 272627*

DOG FRIENDLINESS *Can mostly run free, steps and climbs might not suit some*

PARKING *Roslin Glen Country Park car park*

PUBLIC TOILETS *None en route; nearest at Rosslyn Chapel Visitor Centre*

Despite the splendour of its lush woodland, gurgling waters and delicate wild flowers, the most striking feature of romantic Rosslyn Glen is artificial rather than natural. It's Rosslyn Chapel, the exquisite little church that you meet right at the end of this walk. Founded in 1446 by Sir William St Clair, it took 40 years to build and was originally intended to be a much larger structure.

Curious Carvings

The interior of the chapel is full of intricate stone carvings, created by foreign masons commissioned by Sir William, who supervised much of the work himself. The carvings are not just rich in biblical imagery, as you might expect, but also depict masonic and pagan symbols. For instance, there are over one hundred images of the 'green man', the pagan figure that once symbolised great goodness and fertility – as well as great evil. There is also a depiction of a *danse macabre*, an allegorical representation of death's supremacy over mankind.

Crime of Passion

Perhaps the most stunning carving in the chapel is the Apprentice Pillar, an extraordinarily ornate piece of work. It is said that the pillar was carved by a talented apprentice while his master was away. When the master mason returned he was so jealous of the beauty and craftsmanship of the work that he killed the boy in a fit of jealousy.

The Knights Templar

Rosslyn's greatest mysteries come from its associations with the Knights Templar, the medieval order of warrior monks. They were originally formed to protect pilgrims travelling to the Holy Land – and one of their founders was married to a relative of Sir William. The Templars became immensely wealthy and powerful and were eventually persecuted, being accused of immorality and even pagan idolatry. Many fled to Scotland, with help from the freemasons, taking their treasures with them.

Left: Ornate medieval stonework adorns the interior of Rosslyn Chapel (Walk 22)

ROSLIN

The St Clairs have strong masonic links and Rosslyn Chapel is said to have been built as a memorial to the Templars. Some archaeologists think it hides many of their treasures, such as ancient scrolls from Jerusalem, jewels, perhaps the Holy Grail. Some have even speculated that under the Apprentice Pillar is buried the skull of Christ. This little chapel is certainly full of secrets.

Film buffs will also note that Rosslyn Chapel starred as a crucial location in *The Da Vinci Code*.

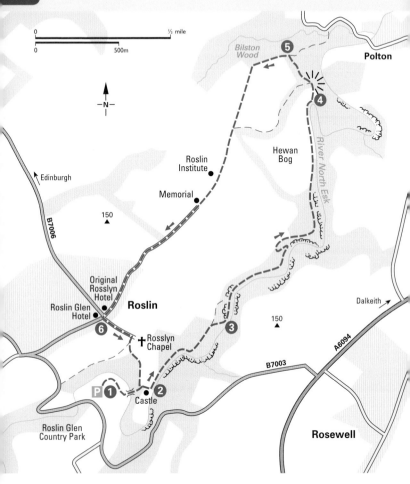

WALK 22 DIRECTIONS

❶ From the country park car park, walk north-east with the sound of the river through the trees to your left. Go up the metal stairs, cross the footbridge, then walk ahead, following the path uphill. In summer, the smell of

wild garlic will soon waft over you. At the bottom of a flight of steps, turn right, walk under the old castle arch, down some stone steps, then turn to your left.

❷ Follow the path through scrub and up some steps into dense woodland. Just by a muddy

burn, bear left, keeping to the main path with the gorge to your right. Beyond a line of yew trees growing from an old stone wall, turn right and follow the path that winds steeply downhill until you reach the water's edge.

WHAT TO LOOK OUT FOR

The memorial to the Battle of Rosslyn commemorates a clash between Scotland and England. The carnage of the fighting gave rise to many local landscape names such as shinbone field, kilburn and stinking rig – a reference presumably to all the dead bodies left in the fields.

3 Walk to your left, then follow the path as it climbs again. At a crossing of paths turn right, following the direction of the river. Your way now takes you high above the river, and you continue ahead to cross a stile. After you cross another stile the view opens out to fields on your left, then takes you closer to the river again, until you reach a kissing gate.

WHILE YOU'RE THERE

Butterfly and Insect World is not far from here at Lasswade, near Dalkeith. It's a great place to bring kids as the enclosures contain loads of beautiful and exotic butterflies in a tropical setting. There are also some separate cages in which an interesting variety of creepy-crawlies are kept.

4 Turn left and follow the path up steps with fields to your left. When you reach the top of the ridge there are good views to your right. Continue until you go through a kissing gate.

5 Turn left and follow the wide path. You eventually walk past buildings of the Roslin Institute, where Dolly the sheep was cloned, then pass a memorial to the Battle of Rosslyn on your right-hand side. Keep walking straight ahead, through the outskirts of Roslin and up to the crossroads at the village centre.

WHERE TO EAT AND DRINK

There's a little café in the visitor centre at Rosslyn Chapel where you can get teas, coffees and cakes. Otherwise there are two reasonable pubs in the centre of the village. The Original Rosslyn Hotel is on your right-hand side as you come into the village and serves bar lunches and high teas. Opposite it, also on the right of your route, is the Roslin Glen Hotel, which also does light bar meals such as baked potatoes.

6 Turn left here and walk ahead. After a short distance you see Rosslyn Chapel on the right-hand side. If you don't intend to visit the chapel, take the path that bears downhill to the right, just in front of it. When you reach the cemetery turn left, following the signpost for Polton, and walk between the cemeteries to the metal gate for Rosslyn Castle. Go down the steps on the right-hand side, over the bridge again and return to the car park at the start.

Edinburgh's Murky Secrets

A stroll through the atmospheric streets of Edinburgh's Old Town.

DISTANCE 2 miles (3.2km)   **MINIMUM TIME** 1hr

ASCENT/GRADIENT 197ft (60m) ▲▲▲   **LEVEL OF DIFFICULTY** ✚✚✚

PATHS City streets, some hill tracks

LANDSCAPE Atmospheric ancient city and brooding castle

SUGGESTED MAP AA Street by Street Edinburgh

START/FINISH Grid reference: NT 256739

DOG FRIENDLINESS Keep on lead, watch paws don't get trodden on by crowds

PARKING Several NCP car parks in Edinburgh

PUBLIC TOILETS At Waverley Station

Edinburgh is often thought of as an extremely respectable, rather genteel city. But as you'll find out in this walk through the city's ancient heart – the medieval Old Town – it has a darker, more mysterious side to its nature.

The Old Town, the original city, was enclosed by city walls, which protected it from the ravages of conflict – but also stopped it from expanding. This meant that as the population grew, the city became increasingly overcrowded, and was at one time the most densely populated city in Europe. The only solution was to build upwards. People lived in towering tenements known as 'lands', with the wealthy taking the rooms at the bottom, the poorer classes living at the top. Its main street, the Royal Mile, became a complicated maze of narrow 'wynds' or alleyways, which gradually deteriorated into a slum. Cleanliness wasn't a priority and residents habitually threw their rubbish into the street – as well as the contents of their chamber pots. When Dr Johnson stayed in the city with James Boswell, he wrote that they had been 'assailed by the evening effluvia' while walking home from a tavern one night.

However, in the progressive 18th century new public buildings were constructed along the steep slopes of the Royal Mile, using the walls of the old slums as foundations. As the city council chambers were extended over the next century, stories were told of cobbled lanes and long-abandoned rooms that still existed deep below in vaulted basements. It wasn't until late in the 20th century that one of these old lanes was opened to the public. Called Mary King's Close, it is full of atmosphere and, as you might expect, is said to be haunted.

Murder in the Dark

There are more dark secrets in the Grassmarket, where the body-snatchers Burke and Hare used to lure their victims before murdering them. They then sold the bodies to a local surgeon who used them in his research. Then there was Deacon Brodie, the seemingly respectable town councillor who had a secret nocturnal life as a criminal and gambler – and was eventually hanged. He was the inspiration for Robert Louis Stevenson's Dr Jekyll, who turned into Mr Hyde, the vicious werewolf, at night. With such a history, it is hardly surprising that crime writer Ian Rankin sets his Inspector Rebus novels in Edinburgh. He often uses gory historical events in his tales, and has plenty to choose from – even an act of cannibalism (*Set in Darkness*, 2000). As Rankin says of Edinburgh – 'It's a very secretive place.'

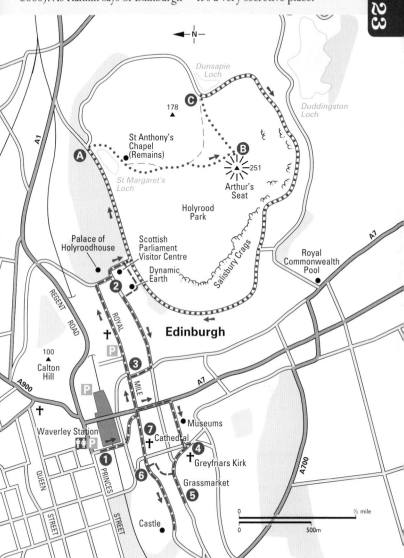

WALK 23 DIRECTIONS

❶ From the main entrance to Waverley Station, turn left, go to the end of the street, then cross over and walk up Cockburn Street to the Royal Mile, where you turn left and walk downhill. Continue to the black gates of Holyroodhouse. Turn right and walk to face the new Parliament visitor centre.

2 Turn left and follow the road to the right, then turn right again past Dynamic Earth (the building looks like a huge white woodlouse) and walk up into Holyrood Road. Turn left, walk past the new buildings of newspaper, *The Scotsman*, and walk up to St Mary's Street, where you turn right and rejoin the Royal Mile. Were you to continue ahead you would join the Cowgate, some parts of which were devastated by fire in December 2002.

3 Turn left, to the main road, then turn left along South Bridge. At Chambers Street turn right and walk past the museums. At the end of the road, cross and then turn left to see the little statue of Greyfriars Bobby, the dog that refused to leave this spot after his master died.

4 You can now cross the road and make the short detour into Greyfriars Kirk to see where Greyfriars Bobby is buried close to his master. Or simply turn right and walk down Candlemaker Row. At the bottom, turn left and wander into the atmospheric Grassmarket – once the haunt of Burke and Hare, it's now filled with shops and lively restaurants.

5 When you've explored the Grassmarket, walk up winding Victoria Street (it says West Bow at the bottom). About two-thirds of the way up look out for a flight of steps hidden away on the left. Climb them and when you emerge at the top, walk ahead to join the Royal Mile again.

6 Turn left to walk up and visit the castle. Then walk down the Royal Mile again, taking a peek into the dark and secretive wynds (alleyways) that lead off it. You eventually pass St Giles' Cathedral on your right, which is well worth a visit if you have time.

7 Next on your left you pass the City Chambers (under which lies mysterious Mary King's Close). Continue until you reach the junction with Cockburn Street. Turn left and walk back down this winding street. At the bottom, cross the road and return to the entrance to Waverley Station.

A Climb to Arthur's Seat

A steep climb gives you great views over Edinburgh.
See map and information panel for Walk 23

DISTANCE 3 miles (4.8km)	**MINIMUM TIME** 1.5hr
ASCENT/GRADIENT 823ft (251m) ▲▲▲	**LEVEL OF DIFFICULTY** +++

WALK 24 DIRECTIONS (Walk 23 option)

This walk starts by the Scottish Parliament visitor centre. The Scottish Parliament was established in 1999, following years of vigorous campaigning by those who wanted some form of self-government. The parliament can pass legislation and also alter the rate of tax. Scotland's former parliament was dissolved when Scotland and England were united in 1707. It had been a rather different institution to the English Parliament and for centuries had done little more than rubber-stamp the monarch's decisions. It did not even have an established home until the end of the 16th century. Many in the parliament supported the loss of Scottish independence, although others saw it as a national tragedy. After union with England, Scotland retained its separate legal and education systems.

From Point ❷ on the main walk, turn left and walk round the side of Holyroodhouse. The Palace of Holyroodhouse is the Queen's official residence while she is in Scotland and was often used by Queen Victoria on her way to Balmoral. It isn't quite as opulent as Buckingham Palace, but has a far more interesting history. Bonnie Prince Charlie held court in the Great Gallery here during the Jacobite rebellion in 1745, and it has strong associations with Mary, Queen of Scots. Her secretary David Rizzio was murdered in front of her in the Royal Apartments – an act believed to have been organised by her husband, Lord Darnley.

At the road turn left and follow it round until you come to St Margaret's Loch (Point ❹). Make your way around the loch and up the steep path to reach the ruins of St Anthony's Chapel. Follow the path as it takes you past the summit on the right-hand side and continue to join a path that comes up from the right. You now follow this clear track up the right flank of a valley to a junction where you bear right to reach the top of Arthur's Seat (Point ❺). This excellent viewpoint is the solidified core of an extinct volcano rising 823ft (251m) above the city. Return to the junction and take the path to the right. Follow it down to Dunsapie Loch and join the main track (Point ❻). Turn right and follow the track all the way round beside the road. Eventually it brings you back to Point ❷, where you turn left and continue on Walk 23.

Go Forth to the Firth

An easy stroll in the shadow of the Forth Bridge — one of Scotland's greatest engineering feats.

DISTANCE 6 miles (9.7km)   MINIMUM TIME 2hr 30min

ASCENT/GRADIENT 197ft (60m) ▲▲▲   LEVEL OF DIFFICULTY +++

PATHS Firm coastal tracks and quiet roads

LANDSCAPE Secluded estuary and historic bridge

SUGGESTED MAP OS Explorer 350 Edinburgh

START/FINISH Grid reference: NT 137784

DOG FRIENDLINESS Keep under close control on Dalmeny estate

PARKING On street in South Queensferry

PUBLIC TOILETS South Queensferry

WALK 25 DIRECTIONS

With your back to the Hawes Inn, cross the road and turn right. Take the tarmac path that runs off to the left, underneath the Forth Bridge. You'll soon get a good view of Inch Garvie Island which was heavily fortified during both World Wars to defend the Forth Bridge and the naval dockyards at Rosyth. The rocks on the left are often dotted with seals, basking in the sun. Keep following the tarmac track and you'll soon get great views of the bridge behind you. Completed in 1890, it took seven years to build and 57 workers died in its making. A mile and a half (2.4km) long and 360ft (110m) high, the bridge was a triumph of Victorian engineering and is considered the 19th-century equivalent of the moon landings.

It was built just a few years after the Tay Bridge disaster. This bridge linked Fife to Dundee and was blown down during a storm, taking with it a train that was crossing at the time and killing 75 people. The tragedy occurred because the builder, Sir Thomas Bouch, had not made allowances for the fierce Scottish winds. Bouch was due to build the Forth Bridge too, but luckily was replaced by Benjamin Baker, the man who created much of the London Underground. Maintaining the bridge against the elements has always been a battle — so much so that painting the Forth Bridge is now synonymous with a task that never ends.

When you reach Long Craig Pier go through a white gate. Keep on the track, passing two cottages. Eventually the landscape opens out and you'll see the large tanker berth out in the Forth. Oil is unloaded here, then pumped to a storage depot near Dalmeny. Your track then runs straight ahead until bearing sharp right at Hound Point. There is a beautiful stretch of sand here and you get a good view of the islands in the Forth. In front of you, towards the Fife coast, is Inchcolm with its ruined medieval abbey. In the middle of the Firth, Inchmickery could be mistaken for a battleship, bristling with gun emplacements and control towers. It is said that

FORTH BRIDGE

the resemblance was deliberately intended as a decoy to lure German submarines into wasting their torpedos on its rocks. Closer in to shore, Cramond Island can be reached at low tide from the pretty village of Cramond, which is well worth a detour on the way back to Edinburgh. The furthest-away island is Inchkeith, which was the setting for a bizarre experiment in the early 1500s when James IV marooned a pair of babies there with a deaf and dumb nurse in order to discover what language they would start to speak – a form of Hebrew apparently.

Your way then takes you past Fishery Cottage on the left-hand side, then through another white gate. At a branching of tracks, maintain direction along the coast to follow the Cramond Walk. Eventually you'll pass the gate to Barnbougle Castle on the left-hand side and your path then leads up to get great views of Dalmeny House, the palatial home of the Earls of Rosebery. It has a large collection of French furniture, tapestries and paintings by Gainsborough,

Raeburn and Reynolds. Bear round to the right, keeping the house on your right hand side, until you reach a crossroads by a statue of a horse. Go straight ahead, following the driveway uphill with railings on your right and continue until you reach the gates at the entrance to the estate. Cross the main road with care and continue walking along the road in front of you. This will eventually bring you into Dalmeny village, which has a lovely little Norman church.

Turn right at the war memorial and walk downhill – you'll see the bridge again. Turn left along Station Road, walk under the railway bridge then turn right immediately to follow the narrow path by the new housing estate. Go up some steps at the end to cross a bridge over an old railway line, which is now a cycleway. Then turn left and walk round the margin of the fenced area (used by the company working on the bridge). When you reach the other side you'll see a long, steep flight of steps running down to the left. Walk down these to come out at the bridge again. Turn left and walk back to the Hawes Inn, where Robert Louis Stevenson stayed while he wrote *Kidnapped*.

Edinburgh's Elegant New Town

A walk in the footsteps
of several literary giants.

DISTANCE *3 miles (4.8km)*   MINIMUM TIME *1hr 30min*

ASCENT/GRADIENT *164ft (50m)* ▲▲▲   LEVEL OF DIFFICULTY ✦✦✦

PATHS *Busy city streets*

LANDSCAPE *Elegant Georgian townscape*

SUGGESTED MAP *AA Street by Street Edinburgh*

START/FINISH *Grid reference: NT 257739*

DOG FRIENDLINESS *Keep on lead, not allowed in Botanic Gardens*

PARKING *Several large car parks in central Edinburgh*

PUBLIC TOILETS *At Waverley Station*

Don't worry, this is not a walk through some dreary 20th-century housing scheme. Edinburgh's New Town was built in the 18th century and is an elegant development of wide airy streets, punctuated with sweeping crescents and lined with soft grey Georgian buildings. It was a planned development, designed to move the focus of the city away from the filthy, overcrowded streets of the medieval Old Town. It was laid out in the mid-18th century by James Craig, a young architect who won a competition for the design. It is separated from the Old Town by Princes Street, the main thoroughfare and once the smartest shopping street in Scotland. In later years Robert Adam contributed to the development, notably designing Charlotte Square in 1791.

Luring the Literati

Houses in the New Town were soon the most coveted in the city and became the haunt of the Scottish literati. Literary associations abound. Kenneth Grahame, author of *The Wind in the Willows* (1908) was born at 30 Castle Street in 1859; Robert Louis Stevenson grew up at 17 Heriot Row; Percy Bysshe Shelley stayed at 60 George Street with his runaway teenage bride in 1811; and Sir Walter Scott once lived at 39 Castle Street.

The city seems to hold a fascination for writers and many historic meetings have taken place here, including that between Sir Walter Scott and Robert Burns. The war poet Wilfred Owen often came into Edinburgh while he was recuperating from 'shell shock' at nearby Craiglockhart War Hospital. One of his early poems was entitled *Six O'clock in Princes Street*. It was at Craiglockhart that Owen met Siegfried Sassoon, already an acclaimed poet, who encouraged him in his writing and made amendments to early drafts of some of his greatest works. Owen left Edinburgh in 1917 and returned to the Front, where he died on 4th November, 1918.

Another New Town location, Milne's Bar on Hanover Street, was a favourite haunt of several of Scotland's most influential modern poets. Hugh MacDiarmid (see Walk 3) and his two friends and drinking partners Norman MacCaig and Sorley MacLean are just some of the figures who used to meet here in the last century, and the pub walls are still covered with their memorabilia.

In the latter stages of this walk you will pass a statue of Sherlock Holmes, a tribute to his Edinburgh-born creator Sir Arthur Conan Doyle, who lived near by at 11 Picardy Place (which has now been demolished). Conan Doyle studied medicine at Edinburgh University and modelled his fictional detective Holmes on one of his former lecturers – Dr Joseph Bell. Bell was an extremely observant individual and combined his instincts with science to help the police in solving several murders in the city. Many believe that Conan Doyle assisted Bell with his work in this capacity – acting as Dr Watson to his Holmes.

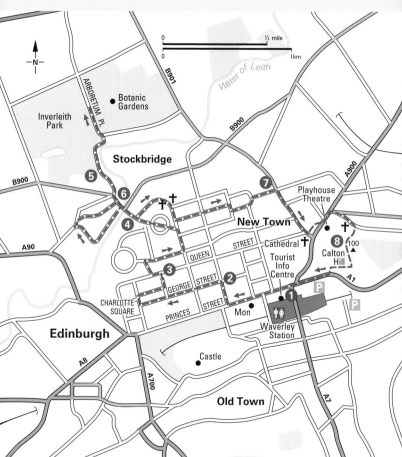

WALK 26 DIRECTIONS

1 From the tourist information centre, turn left and walk along Princes Street. Just after you pass the Scott Monument on your left, cross the road to reach Jenners department store, Scotland's answer to Harrods. Continue along Princes Street, then take a right turn up Hanover Street.

2 Take the second turning on your left and walk along George Street to reach elegant Charlotte Square. Then turn right and right again to go along Young Street. At the end, turn left and walk down North Castle Street to reach Queen Street.

3 Cross the road, turn left, then right down Wemyss Place and right into Heriot Row. When you reach Howe Street turn left and, before the church in the middle of the street, turn left again and walk along South East Circus Place past the sweep of Royal Circus and down into Stockbridge.

4 Cross the bridge, then turn left along Dean Terrace. At the end, turn right into Ann Street. When you reach Dean Park Crescent turn right and follow the road round into Leslie Place and into Stockbridge again. Cross the main road, turn left and then right at the traffic lights down St Bernard's Row. Follow this, then bear left into Arboretum Avenue.

5 Follow this road past the Water of Leith down to Inverleith Terrace. Cross and walk up Arboretum Place to reach the entrance to the Botanic Gardens on the right. Turn left after exploring the gardens and retrace your steps to Stockbridge again.

6 Turn left at Hectors bar and walk uphill, then turn left along St Stephen Street. When you reach the church, follow the road,

cross over Cumberland Street, then turn left along Great King Street. At the end, turn right, then immediately left to walk along Drummond Place, past Dublin Street and continue ahead into London Street.

7 At the roundabout turn right and walk up Broughton Street to reach Picardy Place. Turn left, walk past the statue of Sherlock Holmes, then bear left towards the Playhouse Theatre. Cross over, continue left, then turn right into Leopold Place and right again into Blenheim Place. At the church, turn right, walk up the steps and turn left at the meeting of paths.

8 Go up the steps on the right, walk over Calton Hill, then turn right to pass the canon. Go downhill, take the steps on your left and walk down into Regent Road. Turn right and walk back into Princes Street and the start.

Intoxicating Memories in Leith

A gentle linear walk along the Water of Leith to Edinburgh's ancient port, where claret once flowed in freely.

DISTANCE 3.5 miles (5.7km)   **MINIMUM TIME** 1hr 30min

ASCENT/GRADIENT Negligible ▲▲▲   **LEVEL OF DIFFICULTY** ✦✦✦

PATHS Wide riverside paths and city streets

LANDSCAPE Edinburgh's hidden waterway and revitalised port

SUGGESTED MAP OS Explorer 350 Edinburgh

START Grid reference: NT 243739   **FINISH** Grid reference: NT 271766

DOG FRIENDLINESS Can run free beside water, keep on lead in Leith

PARKING Scottish National Gallery of Modern Art, Belford Road

PUBLIC TOILETS Near Stockbridge

Visitors always forget to come to Leith, yet Edinburgh's ancient seaport is full of history. Even though the docks have been spruced up and become rather trendy, Leith retains an edgy, maritime atmosphere – like an old sea dog who'll spin you a yarn for a pint.

A Taste for Claret

There has been a port at Leith, where the Water of Leith meets the Forth, from at least the 1st century AD when the Romans stored wine for their legions here. The port grew and by medieval times was facilitating valuable trade with France. Ships would leave loaded with dried local fish and return laden with wines, which were landed by the French monks of St Anthony who were based in Edinburgh. One of the main imports was claret. It rapidly became Scotland's national drink, whereas the most popular drink in England was port. One old verse sums up its popularity, beginning with the words: 'Guid claret best keeps out the cauld an drives awa the winter soon'. When cargoes arrived, some would be sent on a cart through Leith and anyone who fancied a sample simply turned up with a jug, which would be filled for 6d. It didn't seem to matter how large the jug was.

Whisky Makes its Mark

The quality of the claret imported and bottled in Leith was extremely good. One historian said it 'held in its day a cachet comparable to that which one now associates with chateau-bottled wines'. Claret drinking was seen as a symbol of Scotland's national identity and Jacobites drank it as a symbol of independence.

During the 18th century the British government, determined to price the French out of the market, raised taxes on claret. Inevitably traders began to smuggle it into Scotland instead. It was only in the 19th century that claret drinking declined when taxes rose and the Napoleonic Wars made it scarce. While Leith claret was still drunk by the wealthiest people, whisky (a drink from the Highlands) took its place as the people's pick-me-up, going from strength to strength to reach its present state of popularity.

79

LEITH

The Port of Leith continued to grow in importance and it was from here, in 1698, that the ill-fated Darien expedition set sail, a venture that was eventually to cost Scotland her independence.

The intention was to establish a permanent colony at Darien on the Isthmus of Panama. It cost £400,000 to fund, but it was thought that the venture would give Scotland control of a potentially lucrative trading route. However the terrain was hostile and the colonists rapidly died. The Scottish economy was plunged into crisis and the country was pushed inexorably towards union with England.

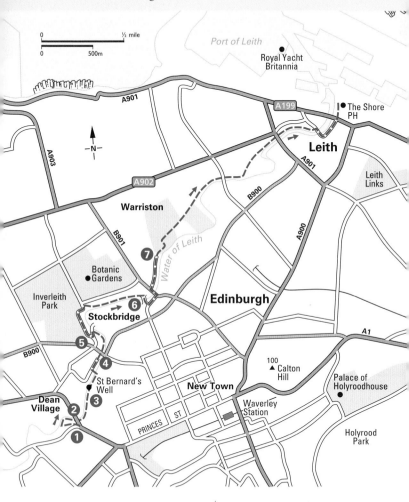

WALK 27 DIRECTIONS

❶ From the junction of the Dean Bridge and Queensferry Street, turn left to walk down Bell's Brae. You are now in the Dean Village, which dates back to 1128. It was once a milling centre and had 11

watermills producing all the meal for Edinburgh. At the bottom, turn right into Miller Row.

❷ Follow this to walk under the impressive arches of the Dean Bridge, which was designed by Thomas Telford and opened in

WHAT TO LOOK OUT FOR

Leith Links is said to be the real home of golf. The rules of the game were established here, only later being formalised at St Andrews. Golf has been played here since the 15th century. In 1641 Charles I was whiling away his time with a round or two when he received the news of the Irish rebellion.

1832. Your path then runs along the bottom of the steeply sided gorge, beside the Water of Leith, and feels extremely rural. You'll pass an old well on your left, followed by the more impressive St Bernard's Well.

WHILE YOU'RE THERE

The former Royal Yacht *Britannia* is moored at Ocean Drive in Leith. It was launched in 1953 and served the Royal Family until 1997, acting as a floating palace and holiday home. Charles and Diana spent part of their honeymoon on the yacht, and the Queen entertained everyone from Bill Clinton to Nelson Mandela. You can go on board the ship and see the accommodation – including the Queen's bedroom, which is surprisingly low-key.

3 St Bernard's Well was discovered by some schoolboys in 1760. The mineral water was said to have healing properties and, in 1789, the present Roman Temple was built, with Hygeia – the goddess of health – at the centre. From here continue along the main path, then go up the steps. Turn left, and go right on to Dean Terrace to reach Stockbridge.

4 Cross the road and go down the steps ahead – immediately to the right of the building with the clock tower. Continue to follow the path beside the river. Where the path ends, climb on to the road, turn left and then right to go down Arboretum Avenue.

5 Walk along this road, then turn right along the path marked 'Rocheid Path'. This runs beside the river and is a popular cycleway and jogging path. Follow this, passing the backs of the Colonies. This low-cost housing was built by the Edinburgh Co-operative for artisans living here in the late 19th century. The idea was to provide houses in a healthy environment away from the dirt of the city. Walk to Tanfield Bridge.

6 Go right, over the bridge, go up the steps, then turn left, walking towards the clock tower. At the end turn left along Warriston Place, cross the road, then turn right down Warriston Crescent. This is lined with town houses. Walk to the end where you'll reach the playing fields.

WHERE TO EAT AND DRINK

Newly gentrified Leith is full of bars and restaurants, many of which are along the water's edge. You can get anything from fish to curry. On sunny days you can sit outside and relax. The oldest pub of all is the King's Wark, which is full of atmosphere and serves good food. Also worth trying is The Shore, a lovely old bar with a separate fish restaurant.

7 Bear right, around the edge of the park, then follow the path as it bears uphill between trees. Turn left at the top and follow the cycle track marked 'Leith 1¼'. Follow this all the way into Leith, where it brings you out near the old Custom House. Cross the bridge, then turn left to walk along the shore and take the chance to explore the pubs, before returning to town by bus.

Overleaf: Rocks on the shallow banks of the Water of Leith at Dean Village (Walk 27)

Poppy Harvest at East Linton

*A delightful and varied walk past an old doo'cot
and a picturesque mill to fields where poppies grow.*

DISTANCE 4.5 miles (7.2km)   **MINIMUM TIME** 2hrs 30min

ASCENT/GRADIENT 295ft (90m) ▲▲▲   **LEVEL OF DIFFICULTY** ✦✦✦

PATHS Field paths, river margins and woodland tracks. Short section of busy road, 3 stiles

LANDSCAPE Cultivated fields, lively river and picturesque village

SUGGESTED MAP OS Explorer 351 Dunbar & North Berwick

START/FINISH Grid reference: NT 591772

DOG FRIENDLINESS Can run free for many sections, watch for sheep though

PARKING Main street in East Linton

PUBLIC TOILETS Pencraig picnic site

If you were to design your ideal walk, what would it include? A dash of history; a crumbling castle; perhaps some fields of waving corn and a peaceful river bank? And maybe a pretty village, in which to settle down finally with a cup of tea and a large wedge of home-made cake? Well, this walk's for you then. It takes you on a lovely varied route through the fertile countryside of East Lothian, just a few miles outside Edinburgh. It's the sort of walk that is enjoyable at any time of year – but it is particularly lovely in the summer when you can see all the wild flowers that line your way.

A Phantastic Doo'cot

The first part of the walk takes you past an old doo'cot (dovecote) where pigeons were bred to be used as food. It once belonged to Phantassie house, a local property which was the birthplace of Sir John Rennie in 1761. Rennie was a civil engineer who, after studying at Edinburgh University, moved to London. There he constructed Southwark and Waterloo bridges, as well as designing dockyards, bridges and canals throughout the country. Not far from the doo'cot is the photogenic Preston Mill, owned by the National Trust for Scotland. This is an 18th-century grain mill and was used to process the produce of East Lothian's fertile arable fields. It has a distinctive conical kiln, which was used for drying the grain, and a barn where the grain was ground. The machinery is driven by a waterwheel.

The Symbolism of Poppies

Later on in the walk, as you make your way towards Hailes Castle, you might well see the scarlet heads of poppies waving among the ripening crops. If you see them on a hot day in August, they make a magnificent spectacle. Sadly, this is a sight you see all too rarely these days, as intensive agriculture has virtually eliminated them from the fields, but it would once have been commonplace. Poppies have been a symbol of blood, harvest and regeneration for thousands of years, as they grow in fields of grain and will rapidly colonise disturbed ground – this was most graphically illustrated in

EAST LINTON

the First World War, and poppies have, of course, also become a symbol of remembrance of lives lost.

Poppies were the sacred plant of the Roman crop goddess Ceres (from whose name we get the word 'cereal'). The Romans used to decorate her statues with garlands of poppies and barley, and poppy seeds were offered up during rituals to ensure a good harvest. Poppy seeds mixed with grains of barley have also been found in Egyptian relics dating from 2500 BC. In Britain it was once believed that picking poppies would provoke a storm and they were nicknamed 'thundercup', 'thunderflower' or 'lightnings'. Whatever you call them, they're a glorious and welcome sight.

WALK 28

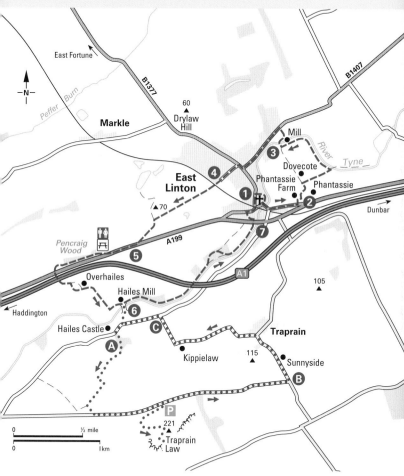

WALK 28 DIRECTIONS

❶ From the Market Cross in the centre of the town, take the lane that runs to the left of the church. When you come to the main street turn left, then walk over the bridge and continue until you reach a garage on the right-hand side. Turn left here into the farm opposite the garage, following the sign for Houston Mill and Mill House.

❷ Follow the path to the right, round the farm buildings until you see the old doo'cot (dovecote)

85

WALK 28

ahead of you. Turn right just in front of it and follow the path along the edge of the field. When you reach the footbridge, turn left to continue walking around the edge of the field, with the river on your right-hand side. At the next footbridge, cross over and go through the metal gate.

❸ Take the right-hand path across the field and go through the kissing gate to reach the old mill. Once you've inspected the mill – you can go inside when it's open – continue on to meet the main road, then turn left to walk back into the town. Turn right to walk along the High Street, then cross over the road and turn left to go down Langside.

❹ When you reach the recreation ground, maintain your direction and walk across the grass to reach the railway. Go through the underpass and walk ahead through the fields. Continue in the same direction, crossing over three walls with the help of some steps and two stiles. After you cross the third wall the track starts to become indistinct, but maintain direction until you come to a footpath sign. Bear left here to reach the road.

❺ Turn right and follow the paved footway through the Pencraig pull-in and on to a signpost to Overhailes. Turn right here and follow it round and under the dual carriageway. From the farm continue down to the end of the lane at Hailes Mill.

❻ Don't cross over the bridge (unless you wish to visit the ruins of Hailes Castle (see Walk 29)) but instead follow the path that runs to the left of the steps. You're now walking along the river's edge on a narrow path. Follow the path to cross a stile, walk along a field margin and under a new road bridge, then enter some woods. Walk up a flight of stairs, then down some steps, and continue following the path to walk under another road bridge.

❼ The path now runs through a garden and on to the road, where you turn right. Walk under the railway bridge, then turn left and return to the starting point of the walk in the town.

And on to Prehistoric Traprain Law

A longer walk to the site of a prehistoric hill-fort.
See map and information panel for Walk 28

DISTANCE *4 miles (6.4km)* **MINIMUM TIME** *2hrs*
ASCENT/GRADIENT *246ft (75m)* ▲▲▲ **LEVEL OF DIFFICULTY** ✚✚✚

WALK 29 DIRECTIONS
(Walk 28 option)

At Point **6** on the main route, cross the bridge over the river and walk up the narrow path – it can get overgrown in summer with nettles and brambles. Continue following the path, bearing right along the road. When you reach Hailes Castle on the right-hand side, take the turning opposite on the left – Point **A**.

Go through the green metal gate and follow the path as it bears right and becomes an enclosed track, with a wall on the left-hand side. Walk until you reach a gate saying 'farm road only', and take the turning on the left, following the right of way. Continue, to go through a gate and join the road, where you turn left. It's a bit of a long tramp now along the road and, though it's not too busy, do keep an eye out for cars.

Eventually you'll reach Traprain Law on the right-hand side. To enjoy the views, make a detour to climb the law, which you reach via a stile. It was the site of a prehistoric hill-fort. In 1919 a deep pit was discovered on the law, filled with an extraordinary collection of 5th-century silver plate, which had been crushed into pieces as if it was going to be melted down. Some think that it

was loot, plundered by the fort's inhabitants from Roman towns.

Otherwise continue along the road, pass the car park on the right-hand side and walk to the junction – Point **B**. Turn left here, walk up past Sunnyside house, then turn left following the sign to Kippielaw. You now continue on this quiet tarmac road, walk past Kippielaw house, then follow the road as it bears right and goes downhill. At the bottom of the hill, Point **C**, turn left and walk back towards Hailes Castle. Turn right just in front of the castle, walk back over the footbridge, then turn sharp right, almost doubling back on yourself to walk along the river and rejoin the main route at Point **6**.

WHAT TO LOOK FOR

Under its Celtic name Dunpender, the hill-fort atop Traprain Law was once the citadel of a powerful Iron Age tribe known to the Romans as the Votadini and to later British writers as the Gododdin, whose lands stretched from the Forth down to the Tyne. Having survived the Roman occupation, the tribe was eventually defeated by the Anglo-Saxon kingdom of Northumbria during the 6th century.

The Romance of Linlithgow

An easy circuit of Linlithgow Loch and memories of a tragic queen.

DISTANCE	3.5 miles (5.7km) **MINIMUM TIME** 1hrs 30min
ASCENT/GRADIENT	Negligible ▲▲▲ **LEVEL OF DIFFICULTY** ✦✦✦
PATHS	Town streets and firm tracks
LANDSCAPE	Romantic loch and bustling town centre
SUGGESTED MAP	OS Explorer 349 Falkirk, Cumbernauld & Livingston
START/FINISH	Grid reference: NT 001771
DOG FRIENDLINESS	Loch popular with dog walkers, keep on lead in town
PARKING	The Vennel car park by The Cross
PUBLIC TOILETS	The Vennel off Linlithgow High Street

WALK 30 DIRECTIONS

This easy walk takes you to a hidden section of the Union Canal, around Linlithgow Loch, and past the romantic ruins of Linlithgow Palace – the birthplace of Mary, Queen of Scots. The walk is suitable for anyone and is particularly good for children.

With your back to The Cross and the magnificent town hall, turn right to walk along the High Street. You'll pass Annet House on your left, home of Linlithgow Museum, and should then turn left to walk up Lion Well Wynd. When you reach the top, turn right for a few paces and then bear left to cross the railway bridge. Turn left on the other side of the bridge and follow the road. You'll get good views over Linlithgow Palace from here. You'll eventually come to an area of grass on the right-hand side, and a 16th-century dovecote on the left. Bear right here for a few paces, then continue ahead and turn right to cross the bridge over the canal. Turn right again to visit the Canal Centre (open

Easter to October). There's a little museum here where you can see old photographs and artefacts associated with the Union Canal. You can take boat trips to visit the new Falkirk Wheel (see Walk 31), which links the Union and Forth and Clyde canals.

Walk back over the bridge and turn right, then sharp left. Walk back on yourself for a few paces then turn right, downhill. Follow this road to walk under the railway bridge and past the station, which is on your right-hand side. Continue ahead to reach the High Street, then turn left and walk back to reach The Cross on your right-hand side. From the Vennel car park by the town hall, walk down the steps at the far end and down to the loch.

Turn right and follow the path – you'll soon see Linlithgow Palace on the right.

Mary, Queen of Scots, was born here in 1542 and inherited the Scottish throne when she was only one week old, after her father James V died a few weeks after facing defeat by the English at the Battle of Solway Moss. Mary is one of the great romantic figures in history and her life was as eventful, and tragic, as an opera. I mean, just listen to this… Sent to France at the age of six to be educated, she was married young to a French prince. Her husband became king, but died soon after. Mary returned to Scotland, fluent in French and Latin – but having probably forgotten her native language. She was married again, this time to Lord Darnley, a vain and weak man. He was manipulated by her enemies into a frenzy of jealousy over her fondness for her secretary David Rizzio – who was murdered before her eyes in Holyroodhouse. Mary realised that she was their real target and escaped, with Darnley, to Dunbar. She later conspired with the Earl of Bothwell to murder her husband. She then married Bothwell, was involved in a battle with her former husband's supporters and was imprisoned on the island of Loch Leven. Later she fled to England and was imprisoned by Elizabeth I, who saw her as a threat to the English throne. Eventually she was executed for treason at

WHAT TO LOOK FOR
You will see plenty of swans on the loch. Once eaten at medieval banquets, the swan is now a protected species. However, they still suffer many losses each year, both from overhead power cables, which are a hazard in flight, and from lead poisoning caused when they swallow lead weights discarded by anglers. Swans mate for life and will grieve deeply when a mate dies. They're extremely territorial and will defend their nests and young vigorously.

Fotheringhay Castle in 1587, wearing a crimson velvet bodice.

When you reach the children's play area continue ahead, then turn right over the little footbridge that leads away from the loch. Walk up the alleyway, then turn left when you reach the road. Walk until you see Barons Hill Avenue on the opposite side. Go through the wooden gate on your left, through a kissing gate and follow the path as it leads back to the loch. Follow the track as it winds round the loch, then go through another kissing gate to reach the road. Turn sharp left and follow the path as it continues round the loch. Continue in the same direction (there are great views of the palace from here) with the loch on your left. Eventually you'll join a tarmac track and come to some houses on the right. Follow the path over another bridge. The path now continues around the loch, then takes you past a parking area on the right and past a fishing lodge. The landing stage is a good place to see the swans that live on the loch. Walk past some modern houses on the right-hand side, and continue following the track until you reach a wall. Turn right here and walk back up into the car park.

WHILE YOU'RE THERE
Not far from Linlithgow at Bo'ness is the Bo'ness and Kinneil Railway, a privately run steam railway. There's a lovely little restored station and several gleaming, restored locomotives and carriages. They run steam trips throughout the year.

Overleaf: Across the lake to Linlithgow Palace, birthplace of Mary, Queen of Scots (Walk 30)

Reinventing the Wheel at Falkirk

*A stroll along Scotland's old canal system to see
a strikingly modern 21st-century wheel.*

DISTANCE	2 miles (3.2km); 4 miles (6.4km) with monument
MINIMUM TIME	1hr
ASCENT/GRADIENT	197ft (60m) ▲▲▲ **LEVEL OF DIFFICULTY** ✦✦✦
PATHS	Canal tow paths and town streets
LANDSCAPE	Roman wall, 19th-century waterways, 21st-century wheel
SUGGESTED MAP	OS Explorer 349 Falkirk, Cumbernauld & Livingston
START/FINISH	Grid reference: NS 868800
DOG FRIENDLINESS	Good along canals
PARKING	Car park at Lock 16, by Union Inn
PUBLIC TOILETS	At Falkirk Wheel Visitor Centre

The words 'new' and 'unique' are rather overused these days. They seem to be applied to everything from shades of lipstick to formulations of engine oil. But this walk gives you the chance to see something that fully deserves the epithet. The Falkirk Wheel, which opened in the spring of 2002, is the world's first rotating boat lift. It was designed in order to reconnect the Forth and Clyde and Union canals, which stretch across the central belt of Scotland, and so restore a centuries-old link between Glasgow and Edinburgh.

Cruising the Canals

The Forth and Clyde Canal, which ran from Grangemouth to Glasgow, was completed in 1790 and made a great difference to the Scottish economy. It opened up a lucrative trading route to America – raw materials could now easily be transported east, while finished products could be shipped west. It also meant that coal extracted from the mines in Lanarkshire could be sent into the newly industrialised areas of Glasgow. The canal was so successful that merchants in Edinburgh soon felt that they were missing out on trade. A plan was devised for another waterway, running from Edinburgh to Falkirk. Work on the Union Canal began in 1818 and a flight of locks was constructed to link it to the Forth and Clyde Canal.

Rise and Fall

The canals were used to transport not only goods but also people. Many preferred to travel by barge than by stagecoach, as they were far less bumpy and decidedly warmer. Night boats even had dining rooms and gaming tables. By 1835 over 127,000 people were travelling on the canal each year. However, shortly afterwards the canal craze began to give way to yet another new innovation – the railways. Train travel, which gained in popularity from the middle of the 19th century, offered cheaper and faster transport, leading to the decline of the canal network. They clung to life until the 1960s, when they were broken up by the expanding network of roads. However, the canals have now been recognised as an important part of Scotland's industrial heritage and are being restored. The Falkirk Wheel was built to replace the original flight of locks, which had been removed in the 1930s, and it's as much a work of art as a feat of engineering. The Wheel lifts boats from one canal to another and is the only rotating boat lift in the world. Made of sharply glinting steel, it's 115ft (35m) high and looks rather like a set of spanners that have fallen from a giant's tool kit. It can carry eight boats at a time and lift loads of 600 tonnes.

An incongruous sight against the gentle tangle of vegetation beside the canal, the Wheel seems to have re-energised the waterways, drawing people to it like a monumental magnet.

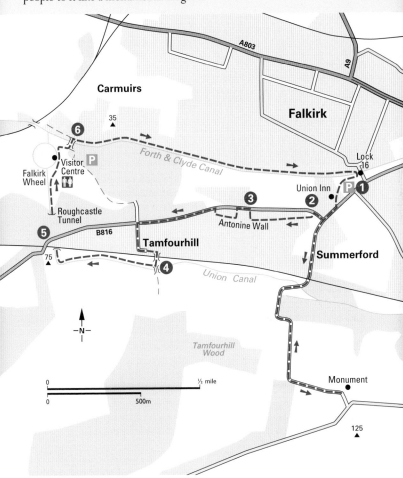

WALK 31 DIRECTIONS

1 Start at the Union Inn by Lock 16. This was once one of the best-known pubs in Scotland and catered for passengers on the canal. Turn right now, away from the canal, then go right along the road. Turn right along Tamfourhill Road and go through the kissing gate on the left-hand side of the road. Alternatively, don't turn up Tamfourhill Road yet, but continue walking uphill to go under the viaduct. Keep walking all the way up until you come to a monument on the left. This commemorates the Battle of Falkirk (1298) in which William Wallace was beaten by Edward I's troops. Retrace your steps, under the viaduct, turn left into Tamfourhill Road, and left through the kissing gate on the left-hand side of the road.

WHAT TO LOOK OUT FOR

Water voles live along the waterways and are often confused with rats. Immortalised by Ratty in *The Wind in the Willows*, voles are a threatened species. They're vegetarians, have a round snout, and are more likely to be spotted during the day than rats (which like to search for food at night).

---

2 This takes you to a section of the Roman Antonine Wall – there's a deep ditch and a rampart behind it. Walk along here, going parallel with Tamfourhill Road. When you reach the point where you can go no further, climb up the bank on the right-hand side and go down the steps to join the road by a kissing gate.

3 Go left to continue along the road – you'll soon see another kissing gate on the left leading you

---

WHERE TO EAT AND DRINK

The Union Inn has a restaurant and beer garden. You can get bar snacks such as filled baguettes, wraps and potato skins or heartier meals like lamb, or trout in lemon butter with almonds. Meals are available both at lunchtime and in the evening. Snacks are available at the Falkirk Wheel Visitor Centre and more substantial meals are served at the Wheelhouse Restaurant.

WHILE YOU'RE THERE

You pass several sections of the Antonine Wall on this walk. It was built in AD 142–3 by Emperor Antonius Pius and stretched for 37 miles (60km), marking the most northerly boundary of the Roman Empire.

---

to another, much shorter, section of the wall. Leave the wall, rejoin the road and maintain direction to reach a mini-roundabout. Turn left here, along Maryfield Place. When you reach the end, join the public footpath signed to the canal tow path and woodland walks. Follow this track as it winds up and over the railway bridge, then on to reach the Union Canal.

4 Don't cross the canal but turn right and walk along the tow path. This is a long straight stretch now, popular with local joggers. Eventually you'll reach Roughcastle tunnel – but remember that it currently closes at 6pm to protect the Wheel from the risk of vandalism.

5 Walk through the tunnel – it's bright and clean and dry. This will bring you out to the new Falkirk Wheel (and yet another section of the Antonine Wall). You can walk on as far as the Wheel, then walk down to the visitor centre at the bottom. Bear right from here to cross the little bridge over the Forth and Clyde Canal.

6 Turn right now and walk along the tow path. Lots of dog walkers and cyclists come along here (so take care if you are walking with a dog), while people frequently go canoeing along the canal. Keep walking until you come back to Lock 16, then turn right and cross the canal again to return to the start of the walk at the Union Inn.

A Leisurely Circuit of Culross

An easy walk that ends on the cobbled streets of an historic town,
where a prosperous trading history is reflected in the buildings.

DISTANCE 3.5 miles (5.7km)   **MINIMUM TIME** 1hr 30min

ASCENT/GRADIENT 180ft (55m) ▲▲▲   **LEVEL OF DIFFICULTY** ✚✚✚

PATHS Generally firm paths, some muddy woodland tracks

LANDSCAPE Ancient town, fields and woodland

SUGGESTED MAP OS Explorer 367 Dunfermline & Kirkcaldy

START/FINISH Grid reference: NS 983859

DOG FRIENDLINESS Can run free on woodland tracks

PARKING Culross West car park

PUBLIC TOILETS By car park in Culross

Walking through Culross is a bit like stepping on to a film set. With its cobbled streets and immaculately preserved buildings, it gives you the impression that you've stepped back in time. The pretty houses, with their red pantiled roofs and crow-stepped gables, give the place a Flemish look, a typical feature of Scottish architecture of this period. Yet despite its neatly manicured appearance, Culross owes its origins to coal mining.

Monks and Miners

The mining industry was started in the 13th century by the Cistercian monks of Culross Abbey, and a flourishing trade soon developed. Coal production allowed a salt-panning industry to grow up, with fires from inferior quality coal being used to evaporate sea water. By the 16th century Culross was one of the largest ports in Scotland, exporting both coal and salt to the Low Countries and the Baltic. On their return journeys they carried red pantiles as ballast – which were used to give the town's roofs their distinctive appearance. There are reminders of these days throughout the town. The area known as the Sandhaven, for instance, which you pass at the end of this walk, was once the harbour. As you pass it, take a look at the Tron, where officials would weigh export cargoes to assess their tax – you can still see the stone platform that supported the weighing beam.

Culross Palace

Trade brought prosperity to the town, as you can see from the many substantial buildings that dot the streets. Most striking of all is Culross Palace, a beautiful ochre-coloured town house. It was built in 1597 by Sir George Bruce, the local bigwig who owned both the mines and the salt pans – the pine-panelled walls, decorative paintings and period furniture reflect the lifestyle of a rich merchant of the period. If you go on a tour, look out for the Flemish-style paintings on the wooden ceiling in the Painted Chamber.

Eventually the industries in Culross died out and the village went to sleep, its period features preserved like those of an insect trapped in amber.

However, in 1923 the palace was bought by the National Trust for Scotland, which then went on to purchase more properties in the village.

As you near the end of this walk, make time to explore. Walking down the hill you'll pass The House with the Evil Eyes – so named because of the shape of its windows – then the church and the remains of Culross Abbey, before coming into the centre of the village. Look for the street known as The Haggs or Stinking Wynd. If you look carefully you'll see that the centre is higher than the edges. This was 'the crown o' the causie', the place where the local toffs walked. The unfortunate hoi polloi had to walk in the gutters – which would have been swimming with – well, you can imagine.

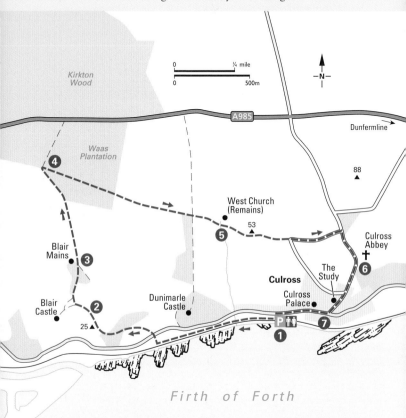

WALK 32 DIRECTIONS

1 From the car park, take steps up to a tarmac path alongside the railway and turn right. Just beyond a reed bed to the right, turn right down some steps and follow the path to the road. Now cross over to the entrance to Blair Castle.

2 Walk up the tarmac drive, which is lined with magnificent rhododendron bushes. Walk ahead until you can see Blair Castle on the left. Before you reach it, take the right-hand turning in the trees and follow it as it bears to the right. Continue until you reach Blair Mains farmhouse, which you'll find on the left.

3 Continue following the track, with fields on either side. Walk ahead until you reach the trees and continue following this track until you reach a metal gate on the left-hand side, just beyond a line of pylons. Look carefully and you should spot a wooden fence post on the right-hand side, with the words 'West Kirk' and 'grave' painted on it in faint white. Take the narrow right-hand path immediately before it, which runs through the trees.

> ### WHILE YOU'RE THERE
> Dunfermline Abbey, in nearby Dunfermline, dates back to the 11th century. The only remains of the original church are the foundations as it was ravaged by raiders many times. It is the burial place of six Scottish kings, as well as Robert the Bruce who is buried beneath the pulpit.

4 Follow this path to go through a kissing gate and continue walking ahead, with trees on your left and fields on your right. Go through another kissing gate, and continue in the same direction. When you reach a crossing of paths, continue ahead along the track and walk under a line of pylons. You will soon pass the remains of a church on the left-hand side.

5 Continue ahead, past the old cemetery, and walk in the same direction until the track joins a tarmac road. Walk in the same direction until you reach a junction. Turn right here and head downhill — watch out for traffic now as the road can be busy. You will soon reach Culross Abbey on the left-hand side.

6 It's worth stopping at this point to visit the abbey. You can then continue to walk on

> ### WHERE TO EAT AND DRINK
> There's a café in the Bessie Bar Hall in the palace where you can get home-made cakes and snacks and hot drinks. Still in Culross, the Red Lion Inn serves a selection of salads, ploughman's and other tasty bar meals.

downhill, down Tanhouse Brae, and will soon reach the Mercat ('old Market') Cross, with The Study on the right-hand side. Continue walking in the same direction, down Back Causeway, until you reach the main road.

> ### WHAT TO LOOK OUT FOR
> The Town House in the Sandhaven was built in 1626 and used to be the seat for local government. The ground floor used to be a prison for debtors, while the attic was used to imprison 'witches'. On one of the houses near by you will find an elegant wall-mounted sundial. Despite the altitude, sundials were highly fashionable in 17th-century Scotland.

7 Turn right, walk past the tourist information centre, past the Tron (the old burgh weighing machine), then past the large ochre-coloured building on the right, which is Culross Palace. To reach the starting point, continue walking in the same direction – the car park is on the left-hand side, just past the children's play area.

Stirling's Braveheart, William Wallace

*Discover the truth about the ultimate
Scottish hero on this town trail.*

WALK 33

DISTANCE 5 miles (8km)   **MINIMUM TIME** 2hrs 30 min

ASCENT/GRADIENT 279ft (85m) ▲▲▲   **LEVEL OF DIFFICULTY** ✦✦✦

PATHS Ancient city streets and some rough tracks

LANDSCAPE Bustling little city topped with magnificent castle

SUGGESTED MAP OS Explorer 366 Stirling & Ochil Hills West

START/FINISH Grid reference: NS 795933

DOG FRIENDLINESS Mostly on lead, not good for those that dislike crowds

PARKING On streets near TIC or in multi-storey car parks

PUBLIC TOILETS At visitor centre by the castle

To many Scots he is the ultimate hero, a charismatic patriot who died fighting for his country's freedom. To others he is less exalted – an outlaw and murderer. Discovering the truth about William Wallace is not easy, as few contemporary accounts exist, although we can be reasonably assured that he didn't look like Mel Gibson or paint his face with woad.

Wallace's heroic status is immediately obvious on your arrival in Stirling, which is dominated by the enormous monument erected in his memory. He was born at Ellerslie near Kilmarnock early in the 1270s and little is known of his early life. He might have remained unknown were it not for the fact that in 1286 the Scottish King, Alexander III, was found dead on the sands at Kinghorn, Fife. His only direct heir was Margaret of Norway – and many powerful Scots did not want a woman on the throne. When Margaret died on her way to Scotland, the succession was plunged into further confusion. The only likely contestants were John Balliol and Robert the Bruce. Edward I was asked to advise, chose Balliol, and then exerted his authority by demanding revenues from Scotland. Balliol later infuriated Edward by signing a treaty with England's enemy, France, and Edward retaliated by sacking Berwick in 1296, slaughtering thousands. The Scots began to resist, Balliol was deposed as king, and the Wars of Independence began.

Wallace Wages War

Wallace joined the struggle. In 1297 he killed the English Sheriff of Lanark and led a number of attacks on English forces. Later that year he won the battle that was to make his reputation, defeating Edward's army at Stirling Bridge. Wallace's forces killed thousands of English and Welsh troops, driving the wounded into the marshes to drown. Wallace now had considerable power. Faced with the possibility of food shortages in Scotland, he ordered an invasion of northern England to plunder food. Many villagers were murdered, churches were burned and over 700 villages destroyed.

In 1298 Wallace was made Guardian of Scotland, but was defeated by Edward I later that year at the Battle of Falkirk. He resigned the Guardianship and travelled to Rome to enlist support from the Pope for the restoration of Balliol as king. Back in Scotland, he continually refused to accept Edward as King of Scotland and was eventually captured and taken prisoner in 1305 (some say he was betrayed by Scots). He was executed at Smithfield in London (the torture of being hung, drawn and quartered was invented for him) and immediately became a martyr for Scottish independence.

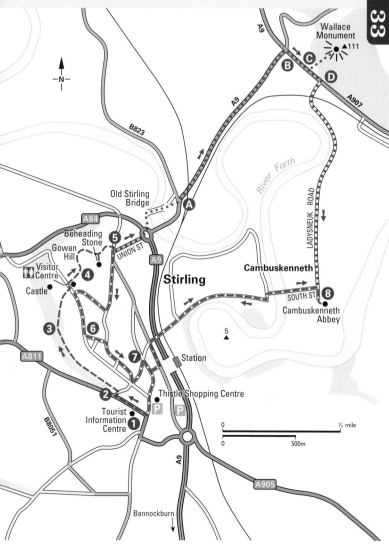

WALK 33 DIRECTIONS

❶ From the tourist information centre on Dumbarton Road, cross the road and turn left. Walk past the statue of Robert Burns then, just before the Albert Halls, turn right and walk back on yourself.

Just past the statue of Rob Roy, turn left and take the path along the Back Wall.

❷ Almost immediately (20yds/18m) turn right up the flight of steps that takes you on to the Upper Back Wall. It's a steady climb now, up past the Church of the Holy Rude, where James VI was crowned in 1567 and on past Ladies' Rock – where ladies of the castle sat to watch tournaments.

3 Continue following the path uphill to reach Stirling Castle. Cross the car park to take the path running downhill just to the side of the visitor centre, so that the castle is on your left. At the cemetery, turn right along the footpath signposted to Moto Hill. Continue up steps and across the cemetery to the gap in the wall.

4 Follow the track downhill on to Gowan Hill. There are several branching tracks but you continue on the main path – heading for the cannons on the hill ahead. At a junction turn right down a track signposted to Lower Bridge Street. Turn on to a grassy slope to the right to see the Beheading Stone. Retrace your steps to the wide track and then follow it to reach the road.

6 Turn left, passing Hermann's Restaurant and the Mercat Cross. Turn right at the bottom down Bow Street, then left along Baker Street. When you reach Friars Street (pedestrianised), turn left and walk down to the end.

> ### WHERE TO EAT AND DRINK
> La Ciociata is a 1950s-style Italian bistro which serves ice creams, cakes, frothy cappuccinos and pizza. Just round the corner is the Barnton Bar and Bistro which serves all-day breakfasts and snacks. For sandwiches, cakes and baked potatoes try Darnley Coffee House – said to have been the home of Lord Darnley, Mary, Queen of Scots' husband.

> ### WHAT TO LOOK OUT FOR
> Stirling Castle was the favourite residence of most of the Stuart monarchs. You can see the interior of the Chapel Royal built by James VI in 1594 for the baptism of his son, and also the restored 16th-century kitchens. You can also see where Mary, Queen of Scots lived.

7 Turn right now, then first left to reach the station. Turn left, then right over the bridge, then bear left in front of a new development to reach the riverside. Maintain direction and join Abbey Road. Bear left at the end, go right over the footbridge and continue along South Street, turning right at the end to visit the remains of Cambuskenneth Abbey.

5 Turn right along Lower Bridge Street, then fork right into Upper Bridge Street. Continue ahead, then 50yds (46m) beyond Settle Inn, turn right up a cobbled lane – it looks a bit like the access to a house. Follow it uphill, then go left at the top. Eventually you'll pass the Castle Esplanade, followed by Argyll's Lodging, and will reach a junction.

8 Retrace your steps back to the station. Turn right, then left, then right again at the Thistle Shopping Centre. Go along Port Street, then turn right along Dumbarton Road to the start.

And Over Stirling Bridge

An extension taking you up to the magnificent Wallace Monument.
See map and information panel for Walk 33

DISTANCE *6 miles (9.7km)*   MINIMUM TIME *3hrs*
ASCENT/GRADIENT *295ft (90m)* ▲▲▲   LEVEL OF DIFFICULTY ✚✚✚

WALK 34 DIRECTIONS (Walk 33 option)

From Point ❺, take the road that runs ahead of you – this is Union Street. Walk to the end to reach a roundabout. Turn left now, then go through the underpass which takes you to the other side of the busy road. Bear right and walk over the attractive bridge ahead of you – this is Old Stirling Bridge, the site of William Wallace's famous victory.

Once over the bridge, bear right to reach the main road (Point Ⓐ) and continue under the railway. It's a long walk now alongside a busy road – it's difficult to imagine what ancient Stirling was like with the cars whizzing past you. However, you'll eventually come to a roundabout (Point Ⓑ) where you turn right to walk along Alloa Road. Just a short distance along on your left is a park and a children's play area. Cross this and you will soon spot some steps in the woods ahead of you (Point Ⓒ).

You can now climb these steps to the top of the crag to reach the Wallace Monument – if you want to climb the monument itself you'll have to pay, but the views on a clear day are great. Walk back down the steps now, across the park, then turn left at the road.

Walk a short distance until you reach Ladysneuk Road (Point Ⓓ). Turn right and walk down here. You'll have to go over a level crossing so cross it with care, then continue along the road. At the bottom, on your left-hand side, you will come to the remains of Cambuskenneth Abbey. After visiting this, rejoin the main walk at Point ❽.

To return to town, walk along South Street, over the footbridge, then bear left and sharp right to walk along Abbey Road, then Shore Road and up over the bridge over the railway. Turn left, walk to the station and continue with Point ❽ of the main walk.

WHILE YOU'RE THERE
The Battle of Bannockburn (1314) is one of the most famous battles in Scottish history and the battle site is not far from Stirling. It was the scene of Scotland's greatest victory over the English, when Robert the Bruce defeated the army of Edward II. It was a victory that was to unite the Scots and led to the Declaration of Arbroath in 1320 – a demand for independence and freedom from English rule. You can visit the heritage centre here and see the statue erected to Bruce.

A Darn Walk from Dunblane

An easy linear riverside walk with memories of Robert Louis Stevenson.

WALK 35

DISTANCE 3 miles (4.8km) **MINIMUM TIME** 1hrs 30 min

ASCENT/GRADIENT 33ft (10m) ▲▲▲ **LEVEL OF DIFFICULTY** ✚✚✚

PATHS Firm tracks and pavements throughout

LANDSCAPE Quiet river banks and small towns, plus grand cathedral

SUGGESTED MAP OS Explorer 366 Stirling & Ochil Hills West

START Grid reference: NS 781009 **FINISH** Grid reference: NS 785977

DOG FRIENDLINESS Good, can run free for much of walk

PARKING By station in Dunblane

PUBLIC TOILETS Near station in Dunblane

WALK 35 DIRECTIONS

This easy walk takes you from Dunblane to Bridge of Allan, following an ancient track beside the Allan Water known as the Darn Road. This is an ancient route and gets its name from the old Gaelic 'Dobhran' or Water Road.

From the station, walk past the Dunblane Hotel to go over the bridge, then turn left down Mill Row. You now follow the wide track that takes you beside the Allan Water. You'll pass a bridge on the left-hand side, and will then continue to walk under a railway bridge. Follow the path until you reach another bridge, where you cross a small burn and take the path that bears right, passing a children's play area. Follow this path uphill until you reach a railway cutting. You'll soon reach some steps on the right-hand side, which take you down to a bridge and across the railway. Your path now continues ahead, taking you over rough ground that in summer is ablaze with pink rosebay willowherb and golden

ragwort. Follow the main track to a fingerpost, signed 'Ashfield 1'. You turn right here, following the edge of the burn until you reach a crossing of tracks. Turn right here and cross the burn, following the track as it now swings up to the road. When you reach the road, turn right. You'll now pass some attractive old weaver's cottages, reminders of the weaving industry that was once so important to this area. Follow the road as it bears to the left and walk straight down to reach Dunblane Cathedral. This was built in the 13th century and is noted for its fine stained-glass windows and carved wood. Most of the medieval stained glass in Scotland was destroyed

WHILE YOU'RE THERE

Sheriffmuir, near Dunblane, was the site of a battle in 1715, when 12,000 Jacobite supporters fought 4,000 government troops in a bid to overthrow the Hanovarian King George I. Although both sides claimed victory, the Jacobites were humiliated by the close result and the rising fizzled out.

DUNBLANE

WHAT TO LOOK FOR

Bridge of Allan was once a small spa town where wealthy people came to drink the curative waters. A large number of properties were built to cater for these visitors, giving the town its prosperous feel. Those taking the 'cure' would drink four pints (2.3 litres) of the water each morning, then relax and explore.

His childhood holidays were spent in Dunblane and he mentions the Allan Water in *Kidnapped* (1886). He later travelled widely and wrote many travel books. He suffered from poor health and moved to Samoa in the hope of benefiting from the climate. He died in 1894, aged just 44.

WHERE TO EAT AND DRINK

The best choice is in Bridge of Allan. The 1950s-style Allan Water Café is very popular with locals for its ice creams and meals such as fish and chips, whilst Clive Ramsay is smart and trendy, specialising in fish dishes along with light snacks.

after the Reformation, so that in the cathedral is of more recent origin. Some of the windows were created by C E Kempe, who is considered one of the finest Victorian stained-glass artists.

After visiting the cathedral, continue walking down to join the High Street and walk up to the Stirling Arms Hotel. Walk ahead, keeping the hotel on your right, and go uphill to reach the main road. Cross the road with care, then take the track almost opposite, next to the bus stop – it's signposted 'Bridge of Allan 2.5'. You're now on the Darn Road. It's a clear track and easy to follow. You'll pass a golf course on the left-hand side and will then go through a wooden gate which takes you into woodland. Eventually you'll come to a footbridge over the Wharry Burn, and then a signpost where you follow the signs for Bridge of Allan. You'll now see the river on your right-hand side. Ignore the footbridge on the right and continue ahead.

You'll soon come to a cave on the left, said by some to be the inspiration for Ben Gunn's cave in Robert Louis Stevenson's *Treasure Island* (1883). Stevenson is one of Scotland's great literary figures and is particularly remembered for his gripping adventure stories.

After this you'll come to some steps, which take you higher above the water. Follow the path downhill and over a footbridge with green railings. Continue to follow the track as it takes you beside pasturelands and then houses, before eventually bringing you up to the main road. Turn right now and walk into Bridge of Allan. Turn left and walk along Henderson Street, the bustling main street which is lined with shops and eating places. At Fountain Road turn right. You will soon come to Holy Trinity Church on the right-hand side, noted for its associations with Charles Rennie Mackintosh. Walk down beyond the fountain, then turn right along Allanvale Road – almost doubling back on yourself. You'll pass some unusual cottages on the right-hand side. Follow this road as it bears round to the right, becoming Union Street, and back on to Henderson Street. You now turn left and walk ahead to cross over the bridge, then turn left down Inverallan Road and bear right to the station to catch the train back to Dunblane.

The Romance of Rob Roy in Callander

*Steep wooded paths lead you through the crags
for superb views of The Trossachs.*

DISTANCE *4 miles (6.4km)* **MINIMUM TIME** *2hrs 30min*

ASCENT/GRADIENT *896ft (273m)* ▲▲▲ **LEVEL OF DIFFICULTY** +++

PATHS *Forest tracks and some rocky paths*

LANDSCAPE *Mixed woodlands, great views of hills and lochs*

SUGGESTED MAP *OS Explorer 365 The Trossachs*

START/FINISH *Grid reference: NN 625079*

DOG FRIENDLINESS *Can run free, steep climb and crags might not suit some*

PARKING *Riverside car park*

PUBLIC TOILETS *Callander*

As you climb through the trees and scramble over the rocks above Callander, it is easy to imagine yourself back in the late 17th century, when Rob Roy and his clansmen lived as outlaws in the heart of The Trossachs. His name has for centuries been tied up with myth and legend, and has inspired authors and film makers – including Sir Walter Scott, who wrote a romantic account of his life in his eponymous novel of 1818. For some, Rob Roy is a Highland hero, for others a notorious cattle thief – whatever the truth behind the myth, he is certainly one of the most colourful characters in Scottish history.

The Wicked Clan Gregor

Rob Roy (the Gaelic for Red Robert) was more properly known as Robert MacGregor. Born in 1671, he was the son of Donald MacGregor of Glengyle. This clan – the 'wicked Clan Gregor' – had been outlawed in 1603, and was known as 'the nameless clan' as they were even forbidden to use their name. The MacGregors had a violent reputation, as they defended their lands and cattle vigorously against assaults from neighbouring clans, which included the rival Campbells, who acted as government agents. Rob Roy, living as a cattle herder in Balquhidder, kept an armed band of men to protect him and his cattle – and extended their services to neighbours who paid him protection money. He began to extend his influence and eventually made a claim to be the chief of the clan.

In 1712, Rob Roy borrowed money from the Duke of Montrose for a speculative cattle deal, and suffered heavy financial losses, which caused a terrible rift between the two men. Rob Roy's lands were seized, his properties plundered and his wife and children were turned out of their home in the middle of winter.

These were already troubled times, for the Jacobite rebellion had begun in 1689 and there were frequent battles between government forces and the supporters of James. Rob Roy, who had fought on the Jacobite side at Sheriffmuir, now gathered his clansmen and took revenge on the Duke of Montrose, supporter of the government.

Loved by the Good

As a result, Rob Roy was outlawed and stories began to appear about his dramatic escapes from his pursuers. He even began to be seen as a sort of Robin Hood figure, generously helping the poor by stealing from the rich. Local people would help him and warn him if troops were in the area.

However, Rob Roy's luck didn't last – he was captured in 1727 and sentenced to transportation. He was later pardoned and went back to Balquhidder, where he seems to have settled down and lived quietly for the rest of his life. He died in 1734 and is buried in Balquhidder churchyard.

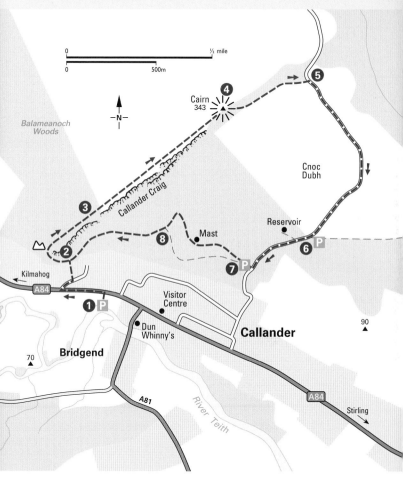

WALK 36 DIRECTIONS

1 From the Riverside car park, walk back to the main road, then turn left. Follow this, then turn right along Tulipan Crescent. Just in front of some modern flats, turn left and follow the wide track. Where the track splits, take the path on the left that is signposted 'The Crags'.

2 Your path now winds steeply uphill through the trees and can get slippery if there's been a lot of rain. Keep following the path and cross a footbridge. Climb to reach a wall on the left-hand side, after which your path narrows. Follow along it to pass a large boulder.

❸ Continue following the path, which eventually bears left, up some steps to a fence. Cross another footbridge, scramble over some rocks and go through a metal kissing gate. You eventually come to a memorial cairn, created in 1897 for Queen Victoria's Diamond Jubilee. On a clear day there are stunning, panoramic views of the surrounding countryside from here.

❹ Leaving the cairn, your path now begins to wind downhill. It's rocky in places and you'll need to take some care as you descend. Follow the path down to the road.

❺ Turn right along the road – you'll see the Wallace Monument near Stirling in the far distance. You'll soon pass a sign on the right-hand side for the Red Well,

where the water runs a distinctly reddish colour owing to the presence of iron traces in the local rock. Continue until you reach a car park on your left. You can make a detour here to see the Bracklyn Falls.

❻ After the car park, stay on the road for about 0.25 mile (400m) passing a track up to a reservoir on your right, then turn right into the Forestry Commission car park (signposted 'The Crags').

❼ Continue to walk through a car park on to a broad Forestry Commission track. Continue walking past the telecommunications mast. At the end of the track, turn left and then walk downhill until you reach a wooden seat and a footbridge.

❽ Take the path that runs to the right of the seat (don't cross the footbridge). Follow the path as it runs downhill and takes you back to the place at which you entered the woods. Turn right, then go left along the main road and walk back into Callander to the car park at the start of the walk.

Academic Traditions at St Andrews

On this easy town trail, discover an ancient university,
which observes some very strange traditions.

DISTANCE *4.5 miles (7.2km)*   MINIMUM TIME *2hrs*

ASCENT/GRADIENT *33ft (10m)* ▲▲▲   LEVEL OF DIFFICULTY +++

PATHS *Ancient streets and golden sands*

LANDSCAPE *Historic university town and windy seascapes*

SUGGESTED MAP *OS Explorer 371 St Andrews & East Fife*

START/FINISH *Grid reference: NO 506170*

DOG FRIENDLINESS *Dogs not permitted on beach*

PARKING *Free parking along The Scores, otherwise several car parks*

PUBLIC TOILETS *Several close to beach*

St Andrews is famous for two things – as the home of golf and of an ancient university. A small town on the Fife coast, it has an atmosphere all its own and feels quite unlike any other town in Scotland.

Reasons for Raisins

The university was established in 1410 and is the oldest in Scotland, and third oldest in Britain – after Oxford and Cambridge. The first faculties established here were theology, canon law, civil law, medicine and arts, with theology being of particular importance. In medieval times students could enter the university as young as 13, and a system of seniority soon arose among the student body. New students were known as bejaunus, from the French 'bec-jaune' or fledgling, and were initiated into the fraternity on Raisin Monday, when they were expected to produce a pound of raisins in return for a cheeky receipt. The tradition persists today, with bejants, as they are now known (females are bejantines), being taken under the wings of older students who become their 'academic parents'. On Raisin Sunday, in November, academic 'fathers' take their charges out to get thoroughly drunk. The next day, Raisin Monday, the 'mothers' put them in fancy dress before they and their hangovers congregate in St Salvator's quad for a flour and egg fight.

Elizabeth Garrett, the first woman in Britain to qualify as a doctor, was allowed to matriculate at St Andrews in 1862 but was then rejected after the Senate declared her enrolment illegal. Following this the university made efforts to encourage the education of women, who were finally allowed full membership of the university in 1892. In 1866 Elizabeth Garrett established a dispensary for women in London, which later became the famous Elizabeth Garrett Anderson Hospital.

Treasured Traditions

The university is proud of its traditions and, as you walk around the streets today, you might well spot students wearing their distinctive scarlet gowns. These were introduced after 1640 and some say they were brightly coloured so that students could be spotted when entering the local brothels. They are made of a woolly fabric with a velvet yoke. First-year students wear them over both shoulders, gradually casting them off each year, until in their fourth and final year the gowns hang down, almost dragging behind them.

Other university traditions include a Sunday walk along the pier after church, which continued until the pier was closed for repair, and a mass dawn swim in the sea on May morning (1 May). Given the icy nature of the waters, this is not an activity to be attempted by the faint-hearted.

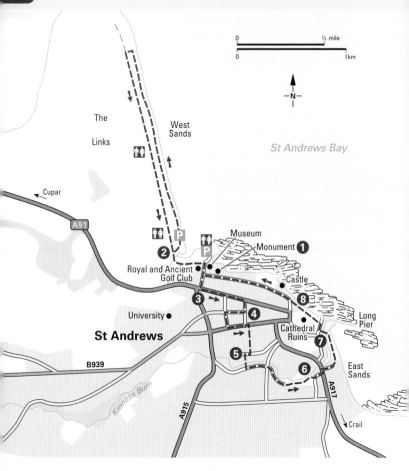

WALK 37 DIRECTIONS

1 With the Martyrs Monument on The Scores in front of you, walk left past the bandstand. At the road turn right, walk to the British Golf Museum, then turn left. Pass the clubhouse of the Royal and Ancient Golf Club on your left, then bear right at the burn to reach the beach.

2 Your route now takes you along the West Sands. Walk as far as you choose, then either retrace your steps along the beach or take one of the paths through the dunes to join the tarmac road. Walk back to the Golf Museum, then turn right and walk to the main road.

3 Turn left along the road and walk to St Salvator's College. Take

a peek through the archway at the serene quadrangle – and look at the initials PH in the cobbles outside. They commemorate Patrick Hamilton, who was martyred here in 1528 – they say students who tread on the site will fail their exams. Now cross over and walk to the end of College Street.

4 Turn right and walk along Market Street. At the corner turn left along Bell Street, then left again on South Street. Opposite Holy Trinity Church, turn right down Queens Gardens to reach Queens Terrace.

5 Turn right then immediately left down steeply sloping Dempster Terrace. At the end cross the burn, turn left and walk to the main road. Cross over and walk along Glebe Road. At the park, take the path that bears left, walk past the play area and up to Woodburn Terrace.

6 Turn left to join St Mary Street and cross over the main road to follow Woodburn Place down

towards the beach. Just before the slipway, turn left along a tarmac path. Cross over the footbridge and join the road.

7 Bear right for a few paces, then ascend the steps on the left. These bring you up to the remains of a church and on to the famous ruined cathedral. A gate in the wall on the left gives access to the site if you wish to visit it.

8 Your route then follows the beachfront past the ancient castle on the right. A former palace/ fortress, it was at the forefront of the Reformation – John Knox preached here. Pass the Castle Visitor Centre, then continue along The Scores to return to the car park at the start.

A Fishy
Trail in Fife

*A linear coastal walk through
the villages of Fife's East Neuk.*

DISTANCE *4 miles (6.4km)* **MINIMUM TIME** *1hr 30min*

ASCENT/GRADIENT *49ft (15m)* ▲▲▲ **LEVEL OF DIFFICULTY** ✦✦✦

PATHS *Well-marked coastal path, 3 stiles*

LANDSCAPE *Picturesque fishing villages and extensive sea views*

SUGGESTED MAP *OS Explorer 371 St Andrews & East Fife*

START *Grid reference: NO 613077* **FINISH** *Grid reference: NO 569034*

DOG FRIENDLINESS *Good, but keep on lead near cattle*

PARKING *On street in Crail*

PUBLIC TOILETS *Route passes plenty both in Crail and Anstruther*

Scotland's James II described the East Neuk (nook) of Fife as 'a fringe of gold on a beggar's mantle'. This corner of the east coast is dotted with picturesque fishing villages, which nestle close together yet retain their own distinctive character.

Crail is perhaps the prettiest village, with a neat little harbour, which attracts many artists and photographers. It was once the largest fishmarket in Europe and, like all the East Neuk villages, used to trade with the Low Countries and Scandinavia; you can see the Dutch influence in the houses with their crow-stepped gables and pantiled roofs.

Further down the coast is Anstruther (known locally as 'Enster'), the largest and busiest of all the villages and home of the local lifeboat. Fishing has always been the focus of life here. The village was the capital of the Scottish herring trade and the harbour was once so busy that you could cross it by stepping over the boats. Look at the houses as you pass and you'll see that many of them have spacious lofts with a pulley outside – designed to store fishing gear and provide an area for mending the nets.

Fishing dominated the lives of people in the past and each of the East Neuk villages was a closely knit community. It was rare for people to marry outside their own village and women were as heavily involved in the work as the men. They prepared the fish, baited the hooks, mended the nets and took the fish to market for sale, carrying enormous baskets of herrings on their backs. They also used to carry their husbands out to sea on their backs so that they could board their boats without getting wet.

Fishing has always had its dangers and many local superstitions are attached to the industry. Women aren't allowed aboard when a boat is working, and it is considered unlucky to utter the word 'minister' on a boat – he had to be referred to as 'the fellow with the white throat' or 'man in the black coat'. Other words to be avoided are 'pig', 'rat' and 'salmon'. These are known as 'curlytail', 'lang-tail' and 'red fish' (or 'silver beastie') respectively. If these words were spoken on a fishing boat the men would cry 'cauld airn' (cold iron) and grab the nearest piece of iron. It's the equivalent of touching wood and is meant to break the bad luck.

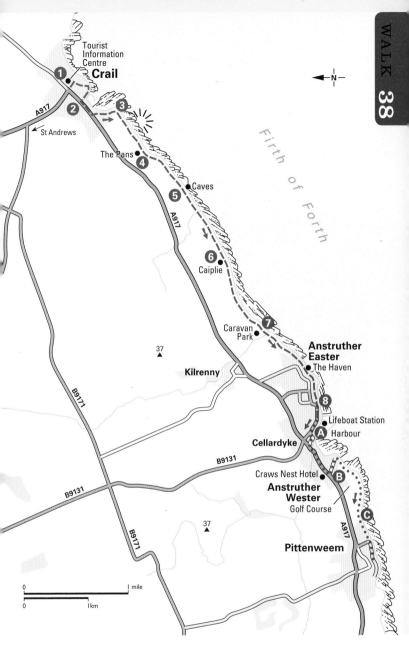

WALK 38 DIRECTIONS

❶ From the tourist information centre in Crail, walk down Tolbooth Wynd. At the end turn right and, where the road divides, you bear left (a sign says 'no vehicular access to harbour'). You'll now be walking beside the old castle wall to a lookout point, which gives you a grand view of the picturesque harbour. Bear right and then walk on to reach the High Street.

❷ Turn left and walk along the road out of the village, passing the two white beacons, which help guide boats into the harbour. Turn left and walk down West Braes, following the signs for the Coastal Path. When you reach Osbourne Terrace turn left down a narrow path, then go down some steps, through a kissing gate and on to a grassy track by the shore.

❸ From here you follow the path as it hugs the shoreline. You should soon see cormorants perched on rocks to your left and will also get views of the Isle of May. Go down some steps, over a slightly boggy area, and continue walking until you reach two derelict cottages – an area known as The Pans.

❹ Walk past the cottages and continue along the shore, then hop over a stone stile. You'll now pass flat rocks on the left, which are covered with interesting little rock pools. Cross the burn by the footbridge – you'll now be able to see the Bass Rock and Berwick Law on your left and the village of Anstruther ahead, and will soon reach some caves.

❺ Pass the caves, then cross a little stone stile on the left-hand side and go over a footbridge. Your track is narrower now and takes you past fields on the right, then some maritime grasses on the left. Stone steps lead to another stile. Climb over it to reach Caiplie.

❻ Go through the kissing gate to pass in front of houses, follow the wide grassy track, then go through another kissing gate to walk past a field. The path now runs past a free-range pig farm and up to a caravan park.

❼ Continue along the shore, on a tarmac track to reach a play area and war memorial on the right. Maintain direction now as you enter the village of Cellardyke and continue to the harbour. Pass the harbour and The Haven restaurant and continue along John Street, then James Street.

❽ At the end of James Street maintain direction, then follow the road as it bends down to the left. You'll walk past a guiding beacon and will come into Anstruther's busy little harbour. You can now either walk back to Crail or take the bus which leaves from the harbour.

And on to be Inspired by Pittenweem

An extension to a busy fishing village where artists abound.
See map and information panel for Walk 38

DISTANCE *1 mile (1.6km)* **MINIMUM TIME** *30min*
ASCENT/GRADIENT *49ft (15m)* ▲▲▲ **LEVEL OF DIFFICULTY** ✦✦✦

WALK 39 DIRECTIONS
(Walk 38 option)

From the Lifeboat Station at the end of Point **8** on Walk 38, continue walking around Anstruther harbour until the main road bears right up Rodger Street (Point **A**) where you maintain your direction to follow the cobbled street ahead. Follow this as it bears right, then turn left at the main road. Walk along the road now, past the Smugglers' Inn, then bear right at the house covered in shells, decorated in this way by its Victorian owner.

You'll walk past the Dreel Burn. This was regularly used by local smugglers, who transported tobacco, cloth, sugar and wine up the burn to trade in Fife, and smuggled linen and coal out.

A plaque at the nearby Dreel Tavern states that James V was carried across this burn by a stout woman when he was travelling incognito through Fife – the local equivalent of Sir Walter Raleigh throwing his cloak over a puddle for Elizabeth I, I suppose.

Follow the road round Dreelside, then turn left just past the Craws Nest Hotel down Bankwell Road (Point **B**). Walk to the end of this road, bear right at the end and walk around the edge of the golf course. You'll soon pass a war memorial on the right-hand side and will then continue following the Fife Coast Path which runs round the edge of the greens – take care in case of stray golf balls.

Eventually you'll reach some stone steps, which you climb up to a seat (Point **C**). Here, bear left with the path, past a field and up to the outskirts of the village. Walk past the children's play area, before bearing left at the end and walking downhill to reach Pittenweem harbour.

This is a busy little place, dominated by the fish market – the village is the hub of the local fishing industry. You can buy fresh fish here to take home, browse round the art shop where paintings by local artists are on sale, or stop for a drink and a snack at the Larachmhor pub. Pittenweem has a reputation as a home and inspiration for artists and holds an Arts Festival every August. To catch the bus back to Crail, walk up from the harbour to the main road.

Reclaimed Land at Lochore

Walk through an area that was once the heart of the local mining industry.

WALK 40

DISTANCE *4 miles (6.4km)*   **MINIMUM TIME** *2hrs*

ASCENT/GRADIENT *66ft (20m)* ▲▲▲   **LEVEL OF DIFFICULTY** ✦✦✦

PATHS *Firm grassy paths and tarmac tracks*

LANDSCAPE *Tranquil loch and mixed woodland*

SUGGESTED MAP *OS Explorer 367 Dunfermline & Kirkcaldy*

START *Grid reference: NS 170962*

DOG FRIENDLINESS *Good, but must stay on lead in some sections*

PARKING *Lochore Park Centre*

PUBLIC TOILETS *Lochore Park Centre*

WALK 40 DIRECTIONS

This easy circuit of Lochore introduces you to an area that provides an excellent example of land reclamation. This is essentially an artificial landscape, for the whole area was once at the heart of the coal mining industry. Large numbers of pits here produced very high-quality coal, which was important to Scotland's industrial success. It was hard, dirty work, which once involved the whole family. Men dug the coal from the ground, while women and children worked behind them in the tunnels. Women would carry the coal to the surface – and the loads were so heavy that it sometimes took two men to lift the basket on to their backs.

From the Park Centre car park, walk towards the loch, bear left in the direction of the green, outdoor pursuits building, then follow the sign to join the footpath that runs round the loch. When you get to the footbridge on your right, cross over and walk through a small patch of woodland. When you reach the wide track, turn right then go through the kissing gate. You're now walking on a broad cinder track and as you walk you'll pass gorse bushes and reed beds – and in summer you may spot dainty harebells too. These are also known as Scottish bluebells and like to grow on poor soils. The path also runs below the cliffs and crags of former quarries, which now have a wild and natural appearance.

Go through a gate, then on through a copse to walk near an island in the lake. The islands are named Moss, Tod and Whaup, taken from old local dialect words for wetlands, fox and curlew respectively. Pass through a series of gates, between fields of grazing cattle and on to a firm track that leads through the woods.

WHERE TO EAT AND DRINK

The Park Centre at Lochore has a small café serving soup and light meals such as baked potatoes and fish and chips, as well as hot drinks and biscuits. It's open from 10:30am to 3pm. If it's a fine day, you can take your own food and have a picnic by the lochside.

LOCHORE

Lochore was originally a boggy meadow, and with the advent of mining became badly scarred by coal 'bings' or spoil heaps, which covered the ground. When the last coal mine closed down in 1967, a programme of reclamation began. One million trees were planted and a huge effort was made to turn the land into an area that could be enjoyed by the local community, who suffered badly after the loss of the mining jobs. The lake was created and gradually wildlife was coaxed into the area.

You'll soon come to a footbridge on your right, which you cross – you can make a short detour if you like by following the track ahead to visit the bird hide. Follow the obvious track (there's a lovely smell of wild thyme in the summer) and the path will then open out on the left-hand side. Go through the metal kissing gate, then turn right to follow the tarmac lane. You soon pass a path off the left which goes to Harran Hill Wood, which is noted for its beautiful carpet of bluebells in spring.

WHAT TO LOOK FOR

You might notice some clumps of wild thyme. This aromatic plant gets tiny purple flowers from May through to August. It can be used in cooking, but you need to use more of it than the variety you grow in your garden as it has a milder flavour.

This wood has an extensive history and may have existed for many centuries. The bluebells, together with the dog's mercury that is also found here, are considered good indicators of ancient woodland. Dog's mercury has male and female flowers on separate plants. It flowers in spring and is poisonous. Wildlife species that live here include wood mice, woodcock

WHILE YOU'RE THERE

Ravenscraig Castle, which is near the Fife town of Kirkcaldy, is a picturesque ruin on the coast. It is said to be the first castle in Britain that was designed to be defended against cannon fire. Steps near the castle lead down to the beach – if you count, there should be 39. They are said to have inspired John Buchan's famous adventure story.

and tawny owls. Woodcocks nest on the forest floor, their plumage cleverly disguising them as a bundle of dead leaves. If you do this walk in the summer you might well notice hundreds of tiny frogs hopping across the path. Although known as the 'common' frog, they are anything but these days, as their numbers have decreased enormously in recent years. Not only do they suffer predation by large numbers of species, ranging from hedgehogs to herons, their habitats have also declined owing to increased drainage of wetlands.

Unless you wish to see the wood, you remain on the tarmac lane. Just beyond a small car park and a barrier pole across the lane, fork right to reach the water's edge. (Alternatively you can keep to the tarmac lane which is the old Pit Road. If you do this, follow the lane to a car park, then turn right to walk back to the visitor centre.) You now walk round the edge of the loch, following the obvious track by the water until you reach the visitor centre and your starting point. The loch is used today for a variety of water sports such as canoeing, kayaking and dinghy sailing. You'll notice winding gear that once served the mines that covered this area.

Along the Tay to Scone

A town trail of Perth with views over Scotland's ancient capital.

DISTANCE 4 miles (6.4km)   **MINIMUM TIME** 2hrs

ASCENT/GRADIENT Negligible **LEVEL OF DIFFICULTY** +++

PATHS City streets and wide firm tracks

LANDSCAPE Historic city and wide, lazy river

SUGGESTED MAP OS Explorer 369 Perth & Kinross

START/FINISH Grid reference: NO 114237

DOG FRIENDLINESS They'll enjoy the river but might not like busy streets

PARKING On street in Perth

PUBLIC TOILETS Off Kinnoull Street in Perth

An ancient description of one of Scotland's most potent symbols – the Stone of Scone, also known as the Stone of Destiny – reads: 'No king was ever wont to reign in Scotland unless he had first sat upon this Stone at Scone.' Scone Palace, of which you get excellent views on this walk, was the crowning place of Scottish kings, including Macbeth and Robert the Bruce. The Stone, which was placed on Moot Hill, by the palace, served as their throne – until it was stolen. The last monarch to be crowned on the Moot Hill was Charles II in 1651 – he was recognised as king in Scotland before he was restored to the throne in England a few years later, in 1660.

Origins of the Stone

Scone was the capital of the Pictish kingdom and was the seat of Kenneth MacAlpin, who united Scotland, from AD 843. The Stone, a piece of red sandstone over 400 million years old, was possibly already in place and could have formed an important part of a pagan ceremony. Geological studies have shown it to be virtually identical to other rocks in the Scone area. The Stone was seen as a symbol of Scotland's nationhood and its significance was to increase after it was stolen by Edward I in 1296. Edward had taken the Stone as a war trophy, determined to exert his authority and crush the independence of the Scots. He had it removed and taken to Westminster Abbey, where in 1297 it was installed beneath the Coronation Chair. Some have claimed that Edward was palmed off with a fake – perhaps even a drainage cover. However this is unlikely, as his officials had already seen the Stone, which has a smooth surface and some distinctive markings.

Return of the Stone

The Scots appealed to the Pope to help them get the Stone returned and, because it apparently had no intrinsic value or aesthetic appeal, the lawyer arguing their case embellished his story of how important it was by claiming that the Stone had been brought to Scotland from Egypt by a pharaoh's daughter. Further myths began to spring up and some even claimed that the Stone was Jacob's pillow.

PERTH

The Stone continued to play its role in history, as all English monarchs from 1297 were crowned upon it. It also continued to be seen as a symbol of Scottish independence and many resented its presence in London. In 1950 some Scottish students managed to steal it from Westminster Abbey, but it was retrieved and replaced. However, in 1996 the Stone was returned to the Scots. It was escorted with due ceremony and put on display in Edinburgh Castle. Many hope that one day it will return to Scone.

WALK 41 DIRECTIONS

❶ From the tourist information centre turn right, then take the first right so you walk round the building. Turn right again and walk down to the road. Cross into Murray Street, passing the bus stops and continue across Kinnoul Street into Mill Street.

❷ Continue down Mill Street, passing Perth Theatre on the right-hand side. Keep walking ahead,

PERTH

WALK 41

pass Caffe Canto (see Where to
Eat and Drink) on the right-hand
side, and join Bridge Lane. You'll
pass the museum and art gallery
on the left-hand side and will
come on to Charlotte Street.
Turn left here.

WHAT TO LOOK OUT FOR

St John's Kirk was founded in
1126 – though most of the
present building dates from the
15th century. It gave the town
its original name 'St John's town'
– now the name of the local
football team, St Johnstone. John
Knox gave a sermon here that
inspired local people to sack the
nearby monasteries.

❸ At the corner you can turn left
if you wish to visit the Fair Maid's
House. Otherwise, cross over the
road and turn right through the
park. Walk past a statue of Prince
Albert then bear left to join the
riverside path. This will give you
good views of the smart houses
along the opposite bank.

❹ Continue ahead on the path,
passing the golf course. When you
reach the sign for the 14th tee,
turn right and follow the track,
with a wall to your left when you
reach the water's edge. You can
either follow the cycle track to the
left of the wall, or walk along the
river bank.

❺ Follow your chosen track until
the two tracks meet, just past an
electricity substation. Walk by the
riverside now to enjoy great views

WHERE TO EAT AND DRINK

Caffe Canto on George Street
is a chic café and a good spot to
enjoy a cappuccino and a cake
or a panini. Pubs worth trying
include the Auld Hoose, Mucky
Mulligan's or the Cherrybank. All
serve bar meals.

of Scone Palace on the opposite
bank – there's a seat so you can
sneak a rest. This is a lovely spot
on a warm, summer's day.

❻ Retrace your steps now,
walking back beside the river or
along the cycle track and back
to the golf course. Turn left and
walk back towards Perth until
you reach the cricket and football
pitches on the right-hand side.

❼ Turn right and walk between
the pitches to join Rose Terrace
where John Ruskin once lived.
Turn left, then bear left at the end
into Charlotte Street and right
into George Street, then right
again into Bridge Lane. Turn left
along Skinner Gate, the site of
the oldest pub in Perth, and walk
along to the end.

WHILE YOU'RE THERE

If you like gardens, make for
Branklyn Gardens on Dundee
Road. This 2-acre (0.8ha) private
garden contains lots of unusual
and rare plants, including
gorgeous Himalayan poppies
– they're the bright blue ones.
There are more plants at Bell's
Cherrybank Centre, the home
of Bell's Scotch Whisky and the
National Heather Collection.
There are over 900 varieties of
heather on display.

❽ Cross over to pass around
St John's Kirk (see What to Look
Out For), through an archway into
South Street and across Princes
Street. At Marshall Place turn left
and walk to the Fergusson Gallery
on the left-hand side. Then turn
back along Marshall Place, walk
up to King Street and then turn
right. Maintain direction now,
then turn left into West Mill Street
and return to the start.

An Ancient Yew in Fortingall

Discover the history of an extraordinary tree on this easy walk amidst stunning mountain scenery.

DISTANCE *3.5 miles (5.7km)*   **MINIMUM TIME** *2hrs*

ASCENT/GRADIENT *33ft (10m)* ▲▲▲   **LEVEL OF DIFFICULTY** ✦✦✦

PATHS *Quiet roads and firm farm tracks, 1 stile*

LANDSCAPE *Picture postcard Scottish scenery, ancient tree*

SUGGESTED MAP *OS Explorer 378 Ben Lawers & Glen Lyon*

START/FINISH *Grid reference: NN 741470*

DOG FRIENDLINESS *Best to keep them on lead in case of cars*

PARKING *Fortingall village*

PUBLIC TOILETS *None en route; nearest in Aberfeldy*

Take a good look at the yew tree in the churchyard at the start of this walk. It is the oldest living thing in Europe – possibly even the world. No one knows exactly how old it is, as yews are notoriously difficult to date (their heartwood dies and they become hollow after around 500 years). However, it is generally reckoned to be around 5,000 years old. Some people think it could even be older – up to 9,000 years. In 1769 the tree's girth was measured and found to be 56ft (17m).

A Special Tree

Long before Christianity, yew trees were held sacred by the Druids and the Celts. This must surely be because of the tree's extraordinary powers of regeneration; they can enter long periods of 'hibernation' when they hardly grow at all – and then suddenly sprout new leaves. Some think yews were planted over graves to protect and purify the dead – others think that sacred sites and burial grounds grew up beside existing yew trees. What is certain is that they have a special place in our culture. Like many pagan symbols, the significance of yew trees was retained and sanctified by the early Christian Church and you will often see yew trees in churchyards today. There are at least 500 churchyards in England and Wales that have yews as old as the church itself, and many of the trees are undoubtedly much older than the building.

Rock a Bye Baby

During medieval times, yews were often placed in churchyards alongside the route that coffins would take. Some think trees were also planted here to provide wood for longbows, while keeping their poisonous branches out of the reach of cattle. The branches of yew trees were also used as church decoration. One famous yew tree in Derbyshire is said to have provided the inspiration for the nursery rhyme 'Rock a Bye Baby'. It's known as the Betty Kenny tree and was once the home of a local family. A child's cradle was created in one of the boughs. Yew trees were also sometimes planted beside inns as a sign to travellers. Two yews were said to indicate that accommodation was available. Three yews meant that the inn was able to make provision for the travellers' animals as well.

Pilate Was Here?

Fortingall is also said to have been the birthplace of Pontius Pilate, who is reputed to have played under the branches of the tree. Apparently Pilate's father was an officer in the Roman army and was stationed here with his wife during the Roman occupation. The family supposedly left Scotland when Pilate was young. However, some claim that Pilate eventually returned to Fortingall and is buried in the churchyard.

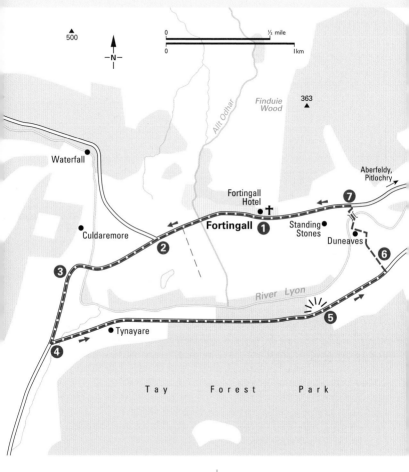

WALK 42 DIRECTIONS

❶ With your back to the Fortingall Hotel, turn right to walk along the road, passing several pretty thatched cottages (an unusual sight in Scotland) on the right-hand side. Follow the road over a burn and then walk past the entrance to Glen Lyon farm. Continue on this road, and eventually you reach a fork in the road.

❷ Ignore the right-hand fork and maintain direction. The road will soon take you over a bridge that crosses the River Lyon.

FORTINGALL

3 Cross over the bridge and continue along the road (it's tarmacked but very quiet), and walk past some little cottages on the right-hand side. Continue until you reach the sign for Duneaves.

WHERE TO EAT AND DRINK

The Fortingall Hotel is a convenient place to get a drink and something to eat – you can sit outside if the weather's good and there are log fires in case it is not. Alternatively, you can make your way into Aberfeldy where there are several pubs and tea rooms.

4 Turn left and follow the road – the river is on your left-hand side. You feel as if you're in a secret valley as you walk along here, and in late summer you can stop to pick the wild raspberries that grow by the roadside. Continue past an area of woodland, after which you get views across the valley to Fortingall.

WHILE YOU'RE THERE

The Birks of Aberfeldy is a beautiful wooded area with a fine circular walk in nearby Aberfeldy. Robert Burns came here in 1787 and was inspired to write a poem on the area. There are many ferns, mosses and trees in the Birks, as well as woodland plants like wintergreen and wood vetch. The woods also provide a habitat for birds including warblers, flycatchers and woodpeckers. It's a walk that children should enjoy.

5 Continue to follow the road until you see a white house on the right-hand side. Leave the metalled track and turn left 50yds (46m) before the house, down a track signposted to Duneaves farmhouse – the views of the surrounding hills are great.

6 Follow the wide, stony track as it leads down to Duneaves. Just before you reach the farmhouse go through the gate in the wall on the right-hand side. Then turn left, following the path around the fields and along the river bank to a rather bouncy footbridge. Bear right after crossing the bridge, then continue through the gate and join the road.

7 Turn left and walk back along the road. You'll soon pass two sets of standing stones in the field on the left – six stones in a ring near the road, and three further away. Walk back into Fortingall to reach your starting place.

WHAT TO LOOK OUT FOR

The wood of yew trees is reputed to outlive iron. A 250,000-year-old yew spear, which was found at Clacton in Essex and is now held at the British Museum, is said to be the world's oldest wooden artefact. Yew wood was traditionally used to make lutes and bows. The earliest records of Yew bows were found during peat extraction in the Somerset Levels and are estimated to be 6,000 years old. Yew tree branches were used to symbolise palms on Palm Sunday.

The Sweet Fruits of Alyth

This varied walk takes you through the fertile heart of Scotland.

DISTANCE 5 miles (8km)	**MINIMUM TIME** 3hrs
ASCENT/GRADIENT 787ft (240m) ▲▲▲	**LEVEL OF DIFFICULTY** +++

PATHS Wide grassy tracks, some rougher paths on hill

LANDSCAPE Mixed woodland, overgrown pasture and gentle hills

SUGGESTED MAP OS Explorer 381 Blairgowrie, Kirriemuir & Glamis

START/FINISH Grid reference: NO 236486

DOG FRIENDLINESS Can run free in many places – keep on lead near sheep

PARKING Car park in Alyth Market Square

PUBLIC TOILETS Alyth Market Square

If you do this walk in the summer or early autumn, put some plastic bowls in the car before you go. That's because Alyth is close to Blairgowrie, and is surrounded by the soft fruit fields of Strathmore. Although you don't pass any strawberry fields on the walk, there are many just a short drive away and you'll see 'Pick your own' signs everywhere.

Fabulous Fruits

This part of Scotland has long been famed for the quality of its soft fruit, particularly its strawberries and raspberries. The land is fertile and the climate mild – perfect for raising sweet, juicy berries. You will see many fields covered in a layer of fine fleece, placed there to protect the strawberry plants, particularly from birds. Fruits from the fields used to be picked to serve the jam-making industry of nearby Dundee. The area's importance for fruit growing is reflected in the names of many varieties of berry. There's the Tayberry (a cross between a blackberry and a raspberry), which refers to the nearby Tay, as well as varieties of raspberry such as Glen Clova and Glen Prosen (both glens being just a short distance from Alyth).

These soft fruits have played an important part in the British diet for a long time, providing valuable vitamin C. Wild strawberries and raspberries are both native to Britain. Strawberries were cultivated in Elizabethan times, although the cultivated ones you buy today are more likely to come from non-native stock: a Chilean species, for example, was introduced in the 1800s and produced larger, more brightly coloured fruits.

Today we tend to use soft fruits for jam or simply eat them fresh or with cream as a treat. However, they were once used in much more complicated recipes. An Elizabethan book, first printed in 1596 and entitled *The Good Huswifes Jewell*, describes a recipe for Tarte of Strawberries that begins: 'Take strawberries and washe them in claret wine, thicke and temper them with rose-water, and season them with cinamon, sugar, and ginger...'

Not only were soft fruits eaten, they were once used to make medicines. Culpeper, the famous 17th-century physician and herbalist, described the versatile healing properties of strawberries in some detail, declaring that the plants were ruled by the planet Venus and that the berries were 'excellent good to cool the liver, the blood, and the spleen, or an hot choleric stomach'. He declared that lotions made from the leaves and roots of strawberries could help ulcers in the 'privy parts' and were also good 'to fasten loose teeth, and to heal spungy foul gums'. Even today, raspberry leaf tea is recommended as a drink for women in the final stages of pregnancy and during labour, while raspberry vinegar makes an excellent gargle for soothing sore throats.

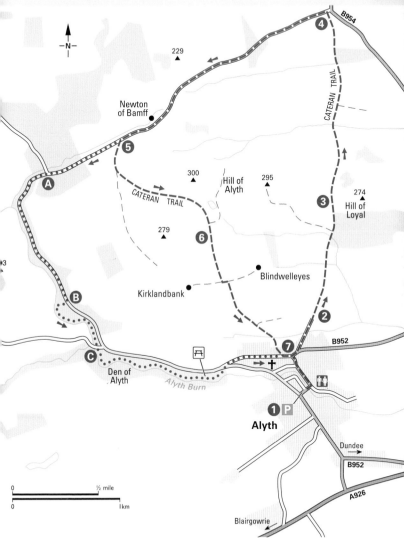

WALK 43 DIRECTIONS

❶ From the Market Square, cross the burn, then turn left along Commercial Street, so that the river is on your left. Turn right up Toutie Street, right again up Hill Street, then left on Loyal Road. Continue walking uphill to reach a sign for the Cateran Trail.

❷ Walk uphill now, go through a gate and continue in the same direction, walking past a wood on the right-hand side. You'll go through a kissing gate, passing an area that in summer is a mass of purple foxgloves. Eventually your path levels out and then starts to bear downhill. Maintain your direction to go through a kissing gate and over a burn.

WHERE TO EAT AND DRINK

The Bridges Coffee Shop in Alyth serves a range of snacks, such as baked potatoes and salads, whilst the Alyth Hotel, also in the Market Square can provide more substantial fare.

❸ From this point the path becomes narrower and bears uphill again, becoming muddier and more overgrown. You'll walk under trees now, through a gate, and will then leave the birch and oak woodland. Keep an eye out for deer here, as you might spot one bounding into the trees, just a few feet away from you. Maintain your direction through the grass, then go through a kissing gate to reach the road.

❹ Turn left and walk along the road, following the signs to the Hill of Alyth Walk. It's pretty quiet along here, so you should meet few cars. The road takes you past a conifer plantation, past a house on the right-hand side and over a cattle grid. Soon after this, you turn left and follow the signs for the Cateran Trail.

❺ Walk uphill and, at a crossing of tracks, turn to the right. Then, within 50yds (46m), turn left uphill. When you reach another crossing of paths, turn right. There are lots of paths traversing the hill, so you can choose your own route at this point, but essentially you must keep the ponds on your left and don't walk as far as the beacon. At the pond, bear right at a waymark sign, aiming for a small copse until you go through a gate.

❻ Walk downhill along the enclosed track – you'll see the spire of the church below you. When you reach another track turn left and then right to continue walking downhill on a metalled track. Walk under a line of pylons and past a farm to eventually reach the village.

WHILE YOU'RE THERE

Explore Alyth, which was once the home of James Sandy. Never heard of him? Well, not only was he the inventor of the invisible hinge (an item we never give a thought to today, probably because it's invisible), but he was also something of a mechanical genius, copying all sorts of items with great success. For some reason he also took to incubating and hatching birds' eggs using the warmth of his body – the young fledglings would then sit on his head and sing.

❼ Your path now bears left along a residential road and takes you downhill. Turn right and retrace your steps along the side of the burn to the start of the walk in the Market Square.

And Through the Den of Alyth

A longer walk by a pretty burn.
See map and information panel for Walk 43

DISTANCE 6.5 miles (10.4km)   **MINIMUM TIME** 4hrs

ASCENT/GRADIENT 558ft (170m) ▲▲▲   **LEVEL OF DIFFICULTY** ✦✦✦

WALK 44 DIRECTIONS
(Walk 43 option)

At Point ❺ on the main route, continue following the road – there are pleasant views on your right-hand side as the ground drops away steeply. Cross a cattle grid and continue ahead with conifers on either side.

The road now winds downhill and brings you to a junction (Point Ⓐ). Turn left here – it's signed 'Alyth 2' – and continue following the road, past Primrose Hill Studio to your right, until you reach a left-hand bend. Just beyond this, take the narrow path that drops steeply down to the right through the trees (Point Ⓑ). When you reach the bottom, go to the left and follow the path that runs by the river. This area is known as the Den of Alyth and is a Site of Special Scientific Interest (SSSI). The area has been wooded for thousands of years and is a mixed wood, with beech, alder, oak, ash and hazel trees.

When you come to a road, maintain direction to go down steps and continue walking beside the river (Point Ⓒ). Follow the path and you'll eventually come to a picnic/ play area on the left-hand side. Continue to walk beside the river until you join the main road. Bear right here and walk along the road to reach the centre of Alyth again.

WHILE YOU'RE THERE

It's worth driving into Dundee, the city on the Tay that is famed in Scotland for the three Js: Jam, Jute and Journalism. The jam industry was supported by the soft fruits grown in the fields around Alyth and nearby Blairgowrie. It was a highly successful industry but began almost by accident. A ship carrying a cargo of oranges took refuge in Dundee harbour during a storm. The fruit could have gone to waste, but an enterprising local grocer bought it and his wife made the oranges into marmalade. Jute, which is made from strong plant fibres, was traded in Dundee from the 19th century and was used to make sacks as well as items such as stage wigs and hair pieces. Dundee's other 'J' – journalism – refers to the presence of the publishers D C Thomson, who still produce newspapers and magazines. Dundee was also an important shipbuilding centre and the home of the *Discovery*, Captain Scott's ship which was launched here in 1901. The ship is moored here today and has a good visitor centre and on-board displays.

Macbeth's Battle at Kinrossie

*An easy walk to the site
of Macbeth's famous defeat.*

DISTANCE 6 miles (9.7km)	**MINIMUM TIME** 2hrs 30min

ASCENT/GRADIENT 591ft (180m) ▲▲▲ **LEVEL OF DIFFICULTY** +++

PATHS Quiet roads, one grassy hill track

LANDSCAPE Quiet villages, fields and historic hills

SUGGESTED MAP OS Explorer 380 Dundee & Sidlaw Hills

START/FINISH Grid reference: NO 188323

DOG FRIENDLINESS No dogs on Dunsinane Hill

PARKING Kinrossie main street

PUBLIC TOILETS None on route

WALK 45 DIRECTIONS

*'Macbeth shall never
vanquish'd be until
Great Birnam wood to
high Dunsinane hill
Shall come against him'*
from *Macbeth,*
William Shakespeare

Well, we all know what happened – in the play, at least. Although Shakespeare's version of Macbeth's life is far from the truth and builds on legends that grew up after his death, there may well have been a battle on Dunsinane (or Dunsinnan) Hill in Perthshire, which is topped with an ancient earthwork. This easy walk takes you to this historic site and gives you the chance to discover the story of the real Macbeth.

From the old cross by the thatched cottage on the main street, walk through the village, keeping the cross on your left-hand side. At the end of the street, turn right along the road signposted 'Collace Church and School'. This is a very quiet road with mature trees on either side. Walk up until you reach Collace church. Just in front of the church, turn right and follow the obvious track past a farm on your left. Continue following it as it narrows (it does get very overgrown in the middle). Eventually the path opens out and you'll come to a road. Turn left and walk down to the junction, then turn left again to follow the road. You'll eventually pass a patch of woodland on your right-hand side and then come to some houses on the left – behind which is the site of an ancient stone circle.

Early sources state that Macbeth was a popular king, 'fair, yellow-haired and tall', who reigned from AD 1040 to 1057. His name MacBeathadh means 'son of life' and he was the son of Findlaech mac Ruaidri, who was the Mormaer (or great steward) of Moray – a title which had the status of an English earl. Macbeth was born at a time when the Scottish succession was flexible and traditionally alternated between relatives and certain clans. The system of primogeniture practised

WHILE YOU'RE THERE

The Meikleour Beech Hedge is a short drive from Kinrossie, on the A93 east of Dunkeld. It's a living wall of glorious beech trees stretching 100ft (30m) high and 0.33 miles (530m) long. Planted in 1745, it is the highest hedge in the world.

in England did not exist and, when a king died, the throne was 'up for grabs'. Macbeth belonged to a clan that had a claim to the throne. In 1020 Findlaech was murdered by three of his nephews, one of whom was later burned to death. Many think Macbeth was involved in this, particularly as he married the dead man's widow Gruoch (the real Lady Macbeth), who had a strong royal pedigree. The marriage certainly strengthened Macbeth's claim to the throne. He became war leader to the young Scottish King Duncan, who reigned for only a few years before he was murdered 'by his own people'. Macbeth has been blamed for his death, too, by one authority. There is little evidence for this, but the murder was to his advantage, for in 1040 he succeeded Duncan as king.

Walk past the pine woods on the left-hand side until you reach a junction. Turn left here – it's signed 'Collace' – and follow the road. It's a pretty quiet road but do keep an eye out for traffic. You'll

pass woods on the left that encircle a hill known as Bandirran Hill. Walk past the quarry entrance on your right-hand side and continue following the road through woodland to a sharp left bend with a gate on the right-hand side. Go through the kissing gate next to the gate (there's a sign saying 'No dogs') and walk up the grassy track, keeping to the fence line on the left-hand side. You'll eventually reach rough moorland where you continue uphill. At the top you come to the ancient fortifications on Dunsinane Hill.

While Macbeth, now king, undertook a pilgrimage to Rome, Duncan's son, Malcolm Canmore, was making plans to avenge his father's death and regain the throne of Scotland. In 1054 he and his troops marched against Macbeth and fought a battle below the royal castle on Dunsinane Hill. Macbeth was defeated and fled to Aberdeenshire, where he was killed by Malcolm in a final battle.

WHAT TO LOOK FOR

If you're interested in Macbeth, it's worth making the journey to Birnam, close to Dunkeld. You can walk from here to see the ancient Birnam Oak. Legend has it that this tree is said to be the last remaining survivor of Birnam Wood, the oak forest mentioned in the play by Shakespeare.

WHERE TO EAT AND DRINK

There's nowhere in Kinrossie but further down the road at Balbeggie is the MacDonald Arms. They've got an extensive menu, and serve bar meals like baked potatoes, fish and chips and toasties, as well as offering more substantial dishes in their restaurant. There are plenty of veggie choices, too.

Retrace your steps to rejoin the road and turn right to walk through Collace village. After the village, keep following the road to reach a junction. Turn left and walk along the narrow road to reach the church again. Turn right, in front of the church, and walk back along the road. At the end, turn left to return to the starting point in Kinrossie.

The Black Gold of the North Sea

A walk around the old fishing port to discover the tragedy and prosperity that oil has brought to Aberdeen.

DISTANCE 3.75 miles (6km)	**MINIMUM TIME** 2hrs
ASCENT/GRADIENT Negligible	**LEVEL OF DIFFICULTY** +++
PATHS Mainly pavements; along beach (underwater at high tide)	
LANDSCAPE Old fishing port	
SUGGESTED MAP OS Explorer 406 Aberdeen & Banchory	
START/FINISH Grid reference: NJ 954067	
DOG FRIENDLINESS Keep on lead	
PARKING Esplanade at Fun Beach or Linx Ice Arena	
PUBLIC TOILETS Upperkirkgate, opposite Marischal College	

Aberdeen was a major maritime centre throughout the 19th century, starting when a group of local entrepreneurs purchased an ageing paddle tug and launched it as the first steam-powered trawler.

From small beginnings the steam trawling industry expanded and by 1933 Aberdeen was Scotland's top fishing port, employing nearly 3,000 men with 300 vessels sailing from its harbour. By the time oil was coming on stream, much of the massive trawling fleet had relocated to Peterhead. An early morning visit to the fish market will verify that Aberdeen still brings in substantial catches, but the tugs, safety vessels and supply ships for the offshore rigs packed into the harbour far outnumber the trawlers.

Black Gold

Geologists had speculated about the existence of oil and gas in the North Sea since the middle of the 20th century, but tapping its deep and inhospitable waters was another story. However, with the Middle Eastern oil sheiks becoming more aware of the political and economic power of their oil reserves and government threats of rationing, the industry began to consider the North Sea as a viable source of oil. Exploration commenced in the 1960s and the first major find in the British sector was in November 1970 in the Forties field, 110 miles (177km) east of Aberdeen.

By late 1975, after years of intense construction, the hundreds of miles of pipes, massive offshore rigs, supply ships, helicopters and an army of oil workers were finally in place. In Aberdeen, at BP's (British Petroleum) headquarters, the Queen pressed the button that would set the whole thing moving. Oil flowed from the rig directly to the refinery at far-away Grangemouth. While many ports have suffered decline, Aberdeen remains busy due to oil trade, as the influx of people connected with the industry and a subsequent rise in property prices have brought prosperity.

The Human Cost

The human cost of oil prosperity was brutally brought home on the night of 6th July, 1988. A huge fire lit the sky as the Piper Alpha oil platform,

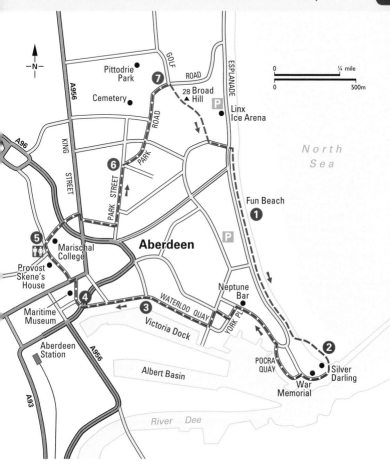

ABERDEEN

120 miles (193km) offshore, exploded. Helicopters flew all night bringing the dead and injured to Aberdeen. In all 167 died; many of the survivors live with the scars of that night and the horrific memories of escaping the burning rig. A memorial to the dead stands in Hazlehead Park. The subsequent inquiry revealed that safety regulations had been ignored. The industry learned a bitter lesson, and the rigs are now safer places to work.

The industry still supports about 47,000 jobs locally and known reserves are such that oil will continue to flow well into the 21st century.

WALK 46 DIRECTIONS

❶ From your parking place, head southwards on the promenade, walking beside the shore with the sea on your left. Go down the slipway on to the beach for a short distance to wooden steps on the right and leave the beach to enter a children's play area. (But if the tide is high at the slipway:

clamber over the sea wall on your right, and pass along a row of fishermen's cottages.)

❷ Walk past the Silver Darling restaurant and into the harbour area. Continue past the war memorial, keeping the blue storage tanks to your left, and along Pocra Quay as it bends right. Turn left into York Street and then at the Neptune bar, turn left into York Place. Take the first right, the first left and second right to emerge on Waterloo Quay.

3 Where Waterloo Quay becomes Commerce Street, turn left into Regent Quay and then at the T-junction cross the dual carriageway at pedestrian lights. Turn left and then first right to reach Aberdeen Maritime Museum and John Ross's House, (he was the Provost of Aberdeen between 1710 and 1711). If you have time, the Maritime Museum is worth a visit.

> **WHILE YOU'RE THERE**
>
> Provost Skene's House, located on Broad Street and passed on route of your walk, is the oldest private dwelling in Aberdeen, dating from about 1545. It was the home of Provost George Skene from 1676 to 1685, and is preserved almost unchanged as a representation of a comfortable 17th-century burgher's residence.

4 From here head along Exchequer Row, to turn left into Union Street. At once turn right into Broad Street, where you will find Provost Skene's House on the left, reached by passing underneath an office block.

5 Now continue ahead past Marischal College (which houses

> **WHERE TO EAT AND DRINK**
>
> If you fancy fish and chips then visit the row of fried-food outlets at Fun Beach.

the Marischal Museum), turn right into Littlejohn Street, and then cross North Street. At the end of Meal Market Street turn right into King Street and then left into Frederick Street. At the junction with Park Street turn left and keep walking ahead until the road crosses a railway.

6 Shortly after the crossing is a roundabout. Head slightly right along Park Road. Follow the road through the Trinity Cemetery and towards Pittodrie Park (the home of Aberdeen Football Club) to the junction with Golf Road.

> **WHAT TO LOOK OUT FOR**
>
> You will see plenty of lichens on this walk, particularly on the last section where they hang from the branches of mature birch trees. Lichens are very sensitive to pollution and don't grow in places where the air is contaminated. This makes them a useful 'indicator species', meaning that their presence or absence tells you something about the environment. The healthy lichens here are a good sign that the air is particularly clear and clean.

7 At the junction with Golf Road, turn up right, on the well-made path over Broad Hill. There are wide views of the sea and Aberdeen. At the path end, turn left to a roundabout with subtropical plants on the Esplanade. The shoreline promenade leads back to your car.

The Inspirational Landscape of Auchenblae

Walk through the fields and woods of the Howe of Mearns, which inspired a Scottish writer.

DISTANCE 6.75 miles (10.9km)   **MINIMUM TIME** 3hrs 30min

ASCENT/GRADIENT 459ft (140m) ▲▲▲   **LEVEL OF DIFFICULTY** +++

PATHS Established footpaths, overgrown woodland tracks

LANDSCAPE Acres of arable fields and cool forests

SUGGESTED MAP OS Explorer 396 Stonehaven, Inverbervie & Lawrencekirk

START/FINISH Grid reference: NO 727787

DOG FRIENDLINESS Fallen trees make it unsuitable except for fit dogs

PARKING On street in Auchenblae

PUBLIC TOILETS Off main street in Auchenblae and at Drumtochty Castle car park

---

'…you'd waken with the peewits crying across the hills, deep and deep, crying in the heart of you … almost you'd cry for that, the beauty of it and the sweetness of the Scottish land and skies'
Sunset Song, 1932

Those words were written by James Leslie Mitchell and sum up the immense love and affection he had for his native Howe of the Mearns in north-east Scotland. It is fertile land, south of Aberdeen. This walk introduces you to this little-walked part of the country, an area that will forever be associated with the author. Mitchell is better known by his pen name of Lewis Grassic Gibbon. He was born in 1901 into a crofting family and had no illusions about the toughness of life on the land. He once wrote: 'My mother used to hap me in a plaid in harvest time and leave me in the lea of a stook while she harvested.' In his books he portrayed the breakdown of crofting life, but did not gloss over its hardships.

Crofter to Author

Gibbon became a journalist at the age of 16 and joined the *Aberdeen Journal*, and later the *Scottish Farmer* in Glasgow. He became ill and moved back home to work in the fields before joining the army as a clerk, later moving into the RAF. He travelled to Central America to see the remains of the Maya civilisation, and later claimed that his digestion was forever affected by the enforced local diet of maize.

Gibbon left the forces in 1929 and returned to Britain, living in the south of England and trying to make his name as a writer. His first book was *Sunset Song*, set in the Howe of the Mearns and telling the tale of Chris Guthrie, who was torn between her desire to escape her small community and her love for the land. He wrote it in six weeks. It was the first of a trilogy, known as *A Scots Quair* (or 'quire' – a volume) and was rapidly followed by the other books *Cloud Howe* (1933) and *Grey Granite* (1934).

AUCHENBLAE

A Short but Prolific Life

Gibbon was extremely disciplined and driven – it was as if he knew he did not have much time to make his name. He divided each day into three and aimed to write 1,500 words in each session. He made some mistakes at first and tried to sell some of his short stories to the wrong type of magazines. However, H G Wells took an interest in his work and suggested different publications for him to try. Lewis Grassic Gibbon eventually died in 1935 of a duodenal ulcer. He was just 34 and had written 16 books.

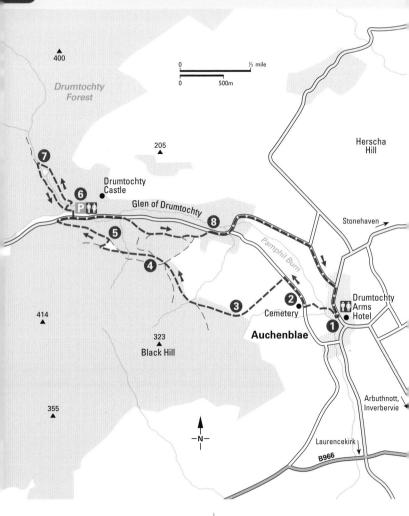

WALK 47 DIRECTIONS

❶ Half-way up the steep High Street, turn left, signed 'Woodland Walks'. The lane runs steeply downhill and crosses Pamphil Burn beside a play area, then runs uphill to a T-junction.

❷ Turn right to walk past a cemetery and then take a grassy track on the left. The track runs up between arable fields to reach the plantation above. Scramble over or past a rusty gate (take care here) and then walk through long grass to reach a track.

AUCHENBLAE

3 Turn right and follow the thickly vegetated track along the bottom edge of the forest. There are a couple of fallen trees to clamber over or walk around. At a wider gravel track, turn right and then continue with fields still visible through the trees below. Above where these fields end, ignore a side-track up left. In another 220yds (200m), fork left on a fainter track.

4 The track runs level then gently uphill. Where a pylon rises on the right-hand side of the track, strike downhill through the cleared ground under the electric wires – this is awkward going, with brushwood underfoot.

5 At the bottom left corner of the cleared ground, a small path strikes left taking you into the forest. The path becomes clearer as it slants gradually down to join the valley road below. Turn sharp right along the road, passing a huge Sitka spruce tree, to Drumtochty car park on the left.

6 Take the track through the car park, bending up left past toilets. After a stiff climb on tarmac, turn right (red waymarker) down a zig-zag path to a mill lade. Turn left along this, to a footbridge above a weir. A little way upstream, the path climbs out of the steep valley, and contours upstream to pass above a small reservoir.

7 At the track beyond, turn left and return to Drumtochty car park. Turn left along the road until a path forks up right past a vehicle barrier. This leads to a forest track, which joins a larger one. Keep ahead, now level, until the track descends left to rejoin the road below.

WHERE TO EAT AND DRINK

The Drumtochty Arms Hotel is a great little pub in Auchenblae village where you can get a drink if you're thirsty. Otherwise try the little village of Inverbervie on the coast, where there are a few places to choose from. There's also a well-known fish and chip shop there called the Bervie Chipper, which has won awards for its food.

8 Turn right and walk along the road, to a junction where you turn left, signed 'Auchenblae', and cross Pamphil Burn. At the following junction bear right, to reach the top end of Auchenblae's High Street.

WHILE YOU'RE THERE

The Lewis Grassic Gibbon Centre is in the village of Arbuthnott, which has strong associations with the author. The centre has displays telling the story of his short but productive life and gives an introduction to the area that inspired his work. In the churchyard you can see the grave marking the place where his ashes were buried. Other places to explore in the Howe of the Mearns include the pretty town of Laurencekirk, close to which is the Hill of Garvock from where you get great views over the land. You can also go to Fettercairn. Among its attractions is the nearby distillery. It's one of the oldest in Scotland.

The Mysterious Stones of Aberlemno

This linear walk takes you through agricultural land once inhabited by the Picts, a fascinating ancient British tribe.

DISTANCE 5 miles (8km)   **MINIMUM TIME** 1hr 45min

ASCENT/GRADIENT 394ft (120m) ▲▲▲   **LEVEL OF DIFFICULTY** ✦✦✦

PATHS Mainly quiet roads but one extremely overgrown area

LANDSCAPE Quiet agricultural land and ancient carved stones

SUGGESTED MAP OS Explorer 389 Forfar, Brechin & Edzell

START/FINISH Grid reference:TQ 522558

DOG FRIENDLINESS Overgrown area makes this unsuitable for dogs

PARKING Car park by school in Aberlemno

PUBLIC TOILETS None en route; nearest in Forfar

Had history turned out differently, you would have been doing this walk in Pictland, not Scotland. The Picts inhabited this northern part of Britain for thousands of years, yet today we know little about them. Neither their language nor manuscripts have survived and their culture remains a mystery. The best reminders we have of them are the intriguing carved stones that dot the landscape of eastern Scotland – the greatest concentration being in Angus and around the Moray Firth. You can see several of these beautiful pieces of ancient art on this walk, which takes you through the heart of the land of the Picts.

The Painted Ones

Mystery surrounds the origins of the Picts. The only thing that seems to be certain is that they occupied what we now call Scotland when the Romans arrived and they may have been here for over a thousand years before that. The Roman Empire soon stretched from southern England to the central belt of Scotland, and the culture and language of the tribes living under the occupation gradually began to alter under their influence. However, the Romans never spread north of the Forth–Clyde line, and so the tribes there kept their distinct language and customs. The Romans called them the Picti, Latin for 'painted ones' – a reference to their warriors' continued habit of daubing themselves in woad, the blue dye from the woad or glastum plant as seen on Mel Gibson's character in the film *Braveheart*.

After the fall of the Roman Empire, new tribes began to invade Britain, with the Angles and Saxons gradually conquering the south, and Gaelic speakers from Ireland, who called themselves Scotti – or Scots – moving into the far north-west.

The Picts were pagans, but they had been exposed to Christian ideas from AD 400 onwards, brought into the country by the great Celtic missionaries Ninian, and later Columba. In AD 565 Columba travelled to Inverness to meet a powerful Pictish king, Bridei. The two men had a competition to see whether Columba's Christian miracles could beat the wiles of Pictish magic. It isn't clear who won, but gradually the Picts converted to Christianity.

ABERLEMNO

Of course there were wars between the various tribes, the Picts fighting the Gaels and Angles, as well as battling among themselves. The carved stone that you pass in Aberlemno churchyard is thought to commemorate one of Bridei's major victories. Stone carving became more and more important in their culture, with increasingly intricate patterns being created, often combined with a Christian cross. However, in AD 794 the Vikings began to raid northern and western Scotland, weakening the Pictish kingdom. The Gaelic-speaking Scots saw their opportunity – in AD 843 a Scot called Kenneth MacAlpin seized their throne, and the Pictish nation died.

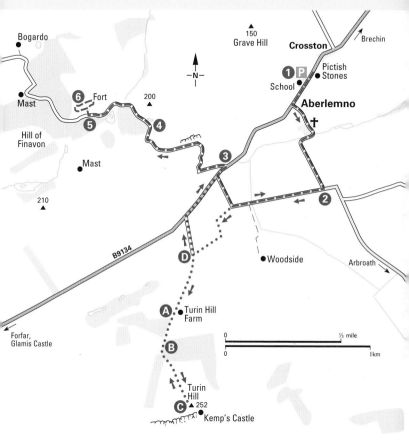

WALK 48 DIRECTIONS

1 From the car park, opposite the Pictish stones, turn right and walk along the road, then go first left, signed 'Aberlemno church and stone'. Walk past the church – another Pictish stone is found in the churchyard – and follow the road as it bends round to the right until you reach a T-junction.

2 Turn right and follow this road, passing the entrance to Woodside on the left. At the corner, follow the road as it bends right. Walk down to join the B9134, turn right and follow this a short distance until you reach a turning on the left.

3 Now turn left along this road, signed 'Finavon Hill'. The

road winds uphill, past several outcrops, then under a line of pylons. Continue on this road as it skirts a hill.

❹ Continue following the road uphill, passing a small loch half-hidden in woodland to the left. Shortly after this, you reach an old stone wall on your right. Just beyond a rusty gate in the corner of a field, you will see a section of the wall has collapsed. Hop over here, taking care to avoid the strand of wire.

❺ Head uphill now to explore the turf-covered ramparts of Finavon vitrified fort. Dating from the Iron Age (1000 BC), the hilltop stronghold had walls built of stones that were fused together by tremendous heat. As you walk around the summit, keep a sharp eye out for vitrified material found in the bank.

❻ From the hilltop, return back down to the road and turn left to retrace your steps back to the start of the walk in Aberlemno.

An Extension to Turin Hill

A longer walk from Aberlemno to an ancient fort.

See map and information panel for Walk 48

DISTANCE *5 miles (8km)*   MINIMUM TIME *2hrs 45min*
ASCENT/GRADIENT *768ft (234m)* ▲▲▲   LEVEL OF DIFFICULTY ✦✦✦

WALK 49 DIRECTIONS
(Walk 48 option)

At the road corner, after passing the entrance to Woodside, take the stony track that bears left. Follow it in front of some farm buildings. When you reach a road, turn left and follow the track past Turin Hill Farm (Point **A**).

Go through a gate and keep ahead across the field. Go through another gate and pass a patch of woodland on the right. Just before a conifer plantation, you reach a wooden gate on the left (Point **B**). Climb this (take care as it may have an electrified wire), before crossing the wooded pasture, keeping the plantation on your right.

Go through another gate and then bear left away from the plantation, climbing uphill to reach a wall on the very top of Turin Hill (Point **C**) with its great views over the surrounding countryside. You can turn left now to see the remains of Kemp's Castle, an ancient fort.

Retrace your steps, back past the wood, across the pasture and over the gates. Walk down to pass the farmhouse again, then keep on the metalled track. Ignore the turning on the right-hand side (Point **D**) and walk ahead to join the main road (the B9134). Turn right and continue until you see a turning on the left signed 'Finavon Hill'. Rejoin the main walk at Point **3**.

WHILE YOU'RE THERE

Arbroath is a short drive from Aberlemno and worth visiting for its famous abbey. This was founded in 1178 by William the Lion and it became an extremely wealthy monastery. It was in the abbey in 1320 that Scottish nobles signed the Declaration of Arbroath, in which Scotland's noblemen affirmed allegiance to Robert the Bruce. The document asked the Pope to reverse its excommunication of Bruce and recognise him as King of Scotland. The document is a clear assertion of Scotland's nationhood and independence from England and contains the famous lines:

'…for as long as but a hundred of us remain alive, never will we on any conditions be brought under English rule. It is in truth not for glory, nor riches, nor honours that we fight, but for freedom — for that alone, which no honest man gives up but with life itself…'

The Pope eventually agreed to their wishes. The words in the Declaration of Arbroath later provided the basis for America's Declaration of Independence.

WALK 50

The Hidden Treasure of Stonehaven

A lovely walk along the cliffs to Dunnottar Castle,
which once housed Scotland's crown jewels.

DISTANCE 3.5 miles (5.7km)	**MINIMUM TIME** 1hr 30min
ASCENT/GRADIENT 377ft (115m) ▲▲▲	**LEVEL OF DIFFICULTY** ✦✦✦

PATHS Cliff edges, metalled tracks, forest paths

LANDSCAPE Striking seascapes, ancient castle

SUGGESTED MAP OS Explorer 396 Stonehaven & Inverbervie

START/FINISH Grid reference: NO 874858

DOG FRIENDLINESS Keep on lead along cliffs

PARKING Market Square, Stonehaven

PUBLIC TOILETS Market Square and harbour, Stonehaven

WALK 50 DIRECTIONS

Scotland's crown jewels are among the oldest in Europe. Also known as the Honours of Scotland, they comprise a crown, a sword of state and a silver sceptre. The crown was created in 1532 for James V. It is made of gold encrusted with precious stones and pearls, and rimmed with ermine. The sword was fashioned in 1507 for James IV and has a silver encrusted scabbard lined with red velvet, while the sceptre, which was made in 1494 and lengthened in 1536, has a pearl-topped globe of rock crystal which some say has magical properties. Together they are powerful symbols of Scotland's independence and can be seen today at Edinburgh Castle, but only thanks to the bravery of the people who hid them from Cromwell's army.

From the Market Square in Stonehaven, walk back on to Allardyce Street, turn right and cross over the road. Turn left up Market Lane and, when you come to the beach, turn right to cross the footbridge. Turn right at a sign to Dunnottar Castle to reach the harbour. Cross here to continue down Shorehead, on the east side of the harbour. Pass the Marine Hotel, then turn right into Wallis Wynd.

WHAT TO LOOK OUT FOR

The pretty little Shell House that you pass in the latter part of this walk was built in the 19th century for the children of the local gentry. It gets its name from the thousands of shells that decorate its interior. A movement sensor means it should light up as you approach close to it.

Turn left into Castle Street which becomes a steep path. You then emerge at the main road and maintain your direction walking along the road until it bends. Continue ahead, following the enclosed tarmac path, between arable fields and past a war memorial on the right-hand side. Cross the middle of the field, then above Strathlethan Bay. The path turns right across the middle of a field and then over a footbridge. You now pass a path going down to Castle Haven and continue following the main path around the cliff edge. Cross another footbridge and bear uphill. You'll soon reach some steps on your left that run down to Dunnottar Castle.

Your walk bears right here inland, past a waterfall, through a kissing gate and then up to a house. Pass the house to reach the road into Stonehaven by the Dunnottar Mains, turn right, then take the first turning left, to walk alongside the farm. Follow this wide, metalled track past East Newtonleys on the left-hand side, to the main A957. Turn right and walk downhill, then take the first road on the left signed 'Dunnottar Church'. Follow this over the Burn of Glaslow to a path on the right signed 'Carron Gate'. Take this path into the woods but at

once fork right, following the lower path that runs by the burn. Continue until you reach the Shell House on the left.

WHERE TO EAT AND DRINK

The Ship Inn by the harbour is a popular spot. You can get substantial dishes such as fish or pasta, as well as toasties. The Marine Hotel nearby serves lunches and supper, as well as coffees. You can also try the Carron Restaurant which has seats outside for fine weather.

Just past the Shell House, continue along the lower path, which then turns uphill to join a higher path. Bear right here, to reach the end of the woods at Carron Gate. You then walk through a housing estate and join Low Wood Road and the River Carron.

Turn left, then right to cross the footbridge with the green railings. Turn right and walk by the water. You'll soon pass the striking art deco Carron Restaurant on the left-hand side, and then come to a cream-coloured iron bridge. Bear left here, then turn first right to return to the Market Square.

WHILE YOU'RE THERE

Visit the Old Church at the tiny village of Kinneff, about 8 miles (12.9km) south, down the coast from Stonehaven. Here you will find the memorial to the Revd Granger and his family, who hid the Honours of Scotland from Cromwell's troops. The Honours are believed to have been placed on both Mary, Queen of Scots and later James VI as babies, so that they could be legitimately crowned. They were also used when Charles II was defiantly crowned King of Scotland in 1651, nine years before he was restored to the English throne. It is often said that some of the gold used in the crown came from the one that belonged to Robert the Bruce.

Walking in Safety

All these walks are suitable for any reasonably fit person,
but less experienced walkers should try the easier walks first.
Route finding is usually straightforward, but you will find that
an Ordnance Survey map is a useful addition to the route maps
and descriptions.

RISKS

Although each walk here has been researched with a view to
minimising the risks to the walkers who follow its route, no walk in
the countryside can be considered to be completely free from risk.
Walking in the outdoors will always require a degree of common
sense and judgement to ensure that it is as safe as possible.

- Be particularly careful on cliff paths and in upland terrain,
  where the consequences of a slip can be very serious.

- Remember to check tidal conditions before walking on the
  seashore.

- Some sections of route are by, or cross, busy roads. Take care
  and remember traffic is a danger even on minor country lanes.

- Be careful around farmyard machinery and livestock, especially
  if you have children with you.

- Be aware of the consequences of changes in the weather and
  check the forecast before you set out. Carry spare clothing and
  a torch if you are walking in the winter months. Remember the
  weather can change very quickly at any time of the year, and
  in moorland and heathland areas, mist and fog can make route
  finding much harder. Don't set out in these conditions unless
  you are confident of your navigation skills in poor visibility. In
  summer remember to take account of the heat and sun; wear a
  hat and carry spare water.

- On walks away from centres of population you should carry a
  whistle and survival bag. If you do have an accident requiring the
  emergency services, make a note of your position as accurately
  as possible and dial 999.

COUNTRYSIDE CODE

- Be safe, plan ahead and follow any signs.

- Leave gates and property as you find them.

- Protect plants and animals and take your litter home.

- Keep dogs under close control.

- Consider other people.

For more information visit www.countrysideaccess.gov.uk/things_
to_know/countryside_code and www.outdooraccess-scotland.com